When God said REMEMBER

Mark Finley

First published in 2010
Reprinted in 2010 & 2011

Copyright © 2010 The Stanborough Press Ltd.

British Library Cataloguing in Publication Data.
Catalogue record for this book is available from the British Library.

ISBN 978-1-904685-80-7

Published by The Stanborough Press Limited, Grantham, Lincolnshire.
Designed by Abigail Murphy.
Printed in Thailand.

Unless otherwise indicated, all texts are taken from the
New International Version of the Bible (Hodder and Stoughton).
Other versions used indicated by initials:
NRSV = *New Revised Standard Version* (Oxford)
NKJV = *New King James Version* (Thomas Nelson)
KJV = *King James Version*

Contents

Before you turn this page

No doubt you have picked up this book because you desire to discover the truth of God's Word. Millions of people just like you are rediscovering the truth about an almost forgotten commandment. A simple reading of the Ten Commandments reveals that the fourth commandment declares, 'Remember the Sabbath day, to keep it holy. Six days you shall labour and do all your work, but the seventh day is the Sabbath of the LORD your God.' (Exodus 20:8-10, NKJV.)

But the majority of the Christian world observes Sunday, the first day of the week, as the Bible Sabbath. Why? Does it make any difference? How did the change of the Sabbath take place from the seventh to the first day? Who changed the Sabbath? Did God give the early Church the authority to change his memorial of Creation?

In an age of growing scepticism and disbelief in the Bible, does the seventh-day Sabbath have any significance today? Has the twenty-first century outgrown the need for the Sabbath? Is a day of rest and worship relevant any longer?

As you read these pages, be prepared for some shocking surprises and straightforward answers. Your traditional beliefs might be challenged. But I am confident that the reason you are reading these pages is because you long for truth. You do not want to be misled by lies. Deep within, you sense the need of finding a rest and peace in the Creator God who made you. As you carefully study the biblical and historical facts in each chapter, you will find rock solid evidence regarding the truthfulness of the Bible Sabbath but, more than evidence, you will find a God who loves you more than you can possibly imagine. You will encounter a loving Creator who values you immensely.

Before you turn this page

The Sabbath will become an island of peace in the storms of life. It will become an oasis to satisfy the inner thirst of your soul. In the Sabbath you will experience God's grace in incredibly amazing ways. You will hear the voice of the One who said, 'Come to me, all you that are weary and are carrying heavy burdens, and I will give you rest.' (Matthew 11:28, NRSV.) In the Sabbath experience you will uncover a rest of mind, body and spirit which will renew and refresh your entire life.

Read on and be prepared to experience a relationship with God in new, exciting ways.

--- Chapter one ---

Rest for the rushed

Do you ever feel that there is just too much to do and not enough time to do it? You feel rushed, pressured and stressed out. However hard you try, you never get caught up on all the things you need to do. There is always one more task, one more item to cross off your 'to do list'.

The tyranny of the urgent consumes your life. You rush from one task to another. And sometimes you wonder, 'Is it really worth it?' Will what I am doing make a lasting difference? Do the things that are most important seem to get pushed out of your life by the things which are the most immediately demanding?

A while back, I came across an interesting newspaper article. Syndicated columnist Arianna Huffington wrote about 'multi-tasking'. That's a phrase that refers to working on several tasks at the same time. More and more we find ourselves 'multi-tasking' in our everyday, personal lives. We try to do two or three things at once. We open our mail and talk to the kids at the same time. We try to carry on a conversation at teatime while watching the evening news. We download our latest emails while talking on the phone with a friend while we are keeping track of our favourite sports team's progress. We eat breakfast in the car on the way to work, listening to the radio and trying to phone our spouse.

Some people even get hooked on multi-tasking. Arianna writes, 'Some of my friends feel alive only when

Rest for the rushed

they are living on the brink, dealing with half a dozen crises, wallowing in the drama of it all and having to drug themselves to sleep.' Add to this frantic pace the stress many people feel from their jobs, and you have a heart attack in the making. In a Study by the National Centre for Health Statistics, half of 40,000 workers surveyed reported 'a lot' to 'moderate amounts of stress in the last two weeks'. A survey by the reputed firm D'Arcy, Masters, Benton and Bowles reveals three quarters of American workers indicate their jobs cause stress. The toll of all this stress is enormous. This year over 1,200,000 people will have heart attacks or severe angina in the United States and over 450,000 will die. Heart disease is America's number one killer. One of the leading causes of death from coronary heart disease is emotional stress. People who are constantly in a hurry, impatient and highly competitive are likely heart attack victims. Drs Ray H. Rosen and Meyer Friedman developed what they termed the 'Type A' personality. This individual tends to be driven by ambition, obsessed with the urgency of time, always under the gun to get things done, highly competitive, never satisfied and continually under stress. Drs Rosen and Friedman's published studies indicate that 90% of heart attacks for men under 60 are in the Type A behaviour category.

In a special medical report on a news channel on 7 January 2008, researchers reported that chronic anxiety could significantly increase the risk of heart attacks, at least in men. 'There is a correlation between the heart and the mind,' said Dr Nieca Goldbery of the New York University School of Medicine. She then added these insightful words, 'Doctors need to do more than prescribe medicine to lower cholesterol and blood pressure . . . they need to deal with the psychological aspect and get into their patients' heads.' Dr BiengJium Shen of the University of Southern California reports in a study on ageing and

heart health that chronically anxious men are 30-40% more likely to have a heart attack than their easygoing counterparts (*MSNBC Medical News*, 7 January 2008).

Escaping the tyranny of the urgent

Is there a way to escape the tyranny of the urgent and move the important things back to the centre of our lives? Is there a way to recapture the vitally crucial things in life? Do you ever feel one day flows into the next, one week flows into the next, and one year flows into the next? How do we stop the rush and find rest for our weary minds and bodies?

I'd like to suggest that God himself has given us a good starting point. He has shown us a meaningful boundary – it is really a place in time. It is a divine space – a timeless symbol of eternity into which he invites us to find renewed peace and rest. We discover this island of peace in the Garden of Eden at Creation.

At the end of the six days of creation week, God instituted the Sabbath. The book of Genesis describes it this way: 'Thus the heavens and the earth were completed in all their vast array. By the seventh day God had finished the work he had been doing; so on the seventh day he rested from all his work. And God blessed the seventh day and made it holy, because on it he rested from all the work of creating that he had done.' (Genesis 2:1-3.) God created 'rest' on the seventh day. The Sabbath is a holy boundary placed in the weekly cycle. It places a pause in the routine of our daily grind. It calls a halt to the rush of our daily work. The Sabbath is God's sacred escape in a frantic world. It is a day set apart from all other days of the week. It is special. It's quality time. It is a time we can reflect on life's most important relationships – our relationship with God and our relationship with our loved ones. And yes, it is a time we can say no to all other demands, all the other things which clutter up our lives.

Human beings desperately need this sacred space –

Rest for the rushed

this divine boundary. We need it more than ever before. The world is busier and noisier and more intense and more demanding than at any time in history. And the Sabbath can keep us from being consumed by it. Rabbi David Wolpe notes, 'The modern world never whispers. Our cities are like arcades without exits. Urgent voices, flashing signs, and an endless stream of media images surround us.' Our overcrowded, overstressed, over-saturated, over-stimulated lives need a rest! We need relief from the constant bombardment of things to find joy in the timelessness of a meaningful relationship with God.

The Sabbath is unique in the whole history of religion. There are many holy things in the religions of the world.

And there are many holy places in the history of the world. Hindus travel thousands of miles to bathe in the sacred waters of the Ganges. Moslems make long pilgrimages to Mecca. Buddhists honour the site where Buddha received the so-called 'enlightenment'. Some Christians travel to Rome or Jerusalem to experience 'sacred presence'.

But in the Bible we find the unique idea of *holiness in time*. God 'blessed the seventh day and made it holy'. God created a holy setting – the Sabbath, where human beings could be specially blessed. But he did not restrict it to a certain location. We don't have to make a long pilgrimage to arrive at God's sacred site. Each Sabbath, Heaven touches Earth. God's eternal place in time descends from Heaven. He has placed his holy setting in time, equally accessible to all humanity. It is a time to find rest in him. It is sacred space in a busy world. It is a divine invitation from the King of the universe to leave the 'rat race' of life to enter the palace of the King.

We are freed from the slavery of our daily work. We are released from the bondage of the earthly to enter into the realm of the heavenly. The Sabbath calls us to

rejoice in his presence. With the psalmist we sing, 'This is the day the LORD has made; let us rejoice and be glad in it.' (Psalm 118:24.)

Sabbath is Heaven's divine invitation to find rest, peace and abundant joy in our loving Creator's presence. It is an invitation to stop rushing and rest. It is Heaven's appeal to place priority on what really matters. It is a weekly reminder that God created us and we belong to him. The Sabbath calls us back to our roots. It reminds us of who we are. It beckons us to a new, meaningful relationship of trust and rest in him.

Spirituality and health

This Sabbath rest renews our relationship with God and our families. It also restores our minds and bodies. God promises: 'Happy is the mortal who does this, the one who holds it fast, who keeps the Sabbath, not profaning it, and refrains from doing any evil.' (Isaiah 56:2, NRSV.) God offers a special blessing to those who set aside time to worship him. Recent scientific studies on religion and health confirm the authenticity of God's promise. The *Instructional Journal of Psychiatry in Medicine* makes this fascinating observation: 'The relationship between religious activities and blood pressure was examined in a six year perspective study of 4,000 older patients. Among subjects who attended religious services once a week or more, and prayed or studied the Bible once a day or more, the likelihood of diastolic hypertension was 40% lower than those who attended services and prayed less often after adjusting for age, sex, race, smoking, chronic illness and body mass index' (pages 189-213). In other words, worship has a positive effect on health. Other studies reveal that a positive worship experience reduces blood pressure, decreases the pain of arthritis and lowers the risk of heart disease. The Sabbath is not a legalistic requirement. It is not some cumbersome burden which weighs us down. Throughout the Old

Rest for the rushed

and New Testaments the Sabbath is a gift from a loving Creator. As we worship the Creator on the Creator's day we are revived, refreshed and revitalised.

Sabbath blessings

The Sabbath is a day of abundant blessings. This is why the Old Testament prophets kept calling people back to God the Creator, to God the lawgiver and to God the deliverer. Here is something these Old Testament prophets repeatedly emphasised: 'Take care that you do not bear a burden on the sabbath day or bring it in by the gates of Jerusalem . . . or do any work, but keep the sabbath day holy, as I commanded your ancestors.' (Jeremiah 17:21, 22, NRSV.)

The prophet Jeremiah speaks about a danger we all face. He discusses a problem for his time but it speaks with relevance to our time. It is not simply a problem for people who lived then; it is a twenty-first-century problem. Here it is. Constant work can squeeze our spirituality. The pursuit of money can eat up all of our time. Seeking the material can crowd out the eternal. It happened in Jeremiah's day in Jerusalem and it is happening in our time in our homes, our workplaces and our cities. And God is saying: 'Let the Sabbath draw you back to what is really important. Don't let the pursuit of material security overwhelm the pursuit of the things that matter most.'

The prophet Isaiah echoes the same theme. Israel was neglecting the Bible Sabbath. Their association with a pagan culture led them to disregard God's special day. In Isaiah chapter 58 God is calling them back to rebuild their faith. He is calling them back to spiritual values. And this is what he says: 'You shall raise up the foundations of many generations; you shall be called the repairer of the breach, the restorer of streets to live in. If you refrain from trampling the sabbath, from pursuing your own interests [business] on my holy day; if you call the sabbath a delight and

the holy day of the Lord honourable; . . . I will make you ride upon the heights of the earth . . .' (Isaiah 58:12-14, NRSV).

Note that those who rebuild the faith were called the repairers of the breach. Obviously there was a breach in the protective wall that surrounded God's people. The Sabbath is a boundary – a wall of protection. It is a place of safety and security. It is part of God's circle of care around us. The Sabbath is a special way for us to experience God's loving, protecting care each week.

Isaiah declares that God promises that, if we honour the Sabbath, the Creator of the universe will cause us to 'ride upon the heights of the earth'. There is richness in Sabbath keeping which leads God's people to prosper physically, mentally, socially and spiritually.

Throughout the New Testament Jesus performed more miracles of healing on the Sabbath than on any other day. He healed a woman afflicted for eighteen years on Sabbath (Luke 13:10-12). He restored sight to a blind man on Sabbath (John 9:1-12). He healed withered arms, palsied bodies and dying children on Sabbath. One of his most spectacular miracles, the healing at the Pool of Bethesda of the man whose body had been diseased for thirty-eight years, was performed on the Sabbath.

What do these Sabbath miracles tell us about Jesus and the Sabbath? They speak of a Christ who longs to give each of his children life in all of its abundance. The Creator re-creates our lives each Sabbath. He restores life in all its fullness each seventh day. The one who made us desires us to be whole physically, mentally and spiritually.

For Jesus the Sabbath was a time for healing. It was a time when people could find relief and rest in him. Jesus wanted to free human beings from the oppressive burdens which crushed out their joy. His attitude towards the Sabbath can be summed up in a simple but profound statement he made in response to

Rest for the rushed

his critics: 'The Sabbath was made for man, not man for the Sabbath. So the Son of Man is Lord even of the Sabbath.' (Mark 2:27, 28.)

Jesus sidestepped ceremony and regulation and showed us a better way to the Kingdom. But he did proclaim himself Lord of the Sabbath. This is significant. To those who think the Sabbath is part of some Old Testament ritual and is a sign of legalism, remember Jesus declared himself Lord of the Sabbath. He says, 'The Sabbath was made for man.' The Sabbath was meant to bless us. The Sabbath was made to benefit us. It is not just another religious obligation. It is not some burdensome requirement. The New Testament Sabbath is a place of grace and rest. It is a place where we renew our relationship with God. It is a place where we find our true centre in him.

In Hebrews chapter 4, the Bible writer quotes from the fourth commandment, the one that commands us to keep the seventh day holy. He reminds his readers that 'on the seventh day God rested from all his work.' (Hebrews 4:4.) Then a few verses later he says, 'There remains, then, a Sabbath-rest for the people of God; for anyone who enters God's rest also rests from his own work, just as God did from his.' (Hebrews 4:9, 10.)

What is this passage of Scripture telling us? It declares we, too, can rest from our labours. We can rest from the oppressive burden of trying to get more and more. We can rest in our Creator's care. The one who made us loves us with an everlasting love. He will care for all our needs. We rest in God's completed work of Creation and redemption. We did not evolve. God created us at a point in time. The Sabbath reminds us that since he made us and fashioned us individually we are special to God. He not only created us, he redeemed us. God worked out our salvation by giving up his Son on the Cross. This great act of grace and acceptance is finished, completed. We don't have to earn it or try to pay God back for it through our good

works. We simply accept it and rest in his love. Each week as we keep the Sabbath it is a symbol that we are safe in the One who created us and in the One who redeemed us.

Sabbath reminds us of the rest we have in Jesus Christ. Each Sabbath we rest from our labours in the supreme acknowledgment that, just as we had no part in Creation, we have no part in earning our salvation. We rest in the grace of the Christ who died for us. Sabbath is a symbol of rest, not work. In Sabbath rest, we rejoice in the one who provides salvation for our guilt-ridden souls.

Sabbath is God's rest for the rushed in a fast-paced world.

Chapter two

Set free to obey

Years ago the home was a place of refuge and security. Down through the centuries it has been a haven of stability. The home was a place to which people could flee from the trials, troubles and difficulties of life. Enter the doors of your home and you feel secure. Warm, loving embraces and hugs produce a sense of well-being. Home has been the traditional place of family togetherness.

The home has changed in the last thirty years. Twenty-first-century homes are often a battlefield.

Words like abuse, conflict, anger and hostility are commonplace when describing the home. We read about families who spend very little time at home. Children often eat on the run. Many families no longer enjoy a family meal together.

At best they rush home for a meal before they leave again. The home has become simply a place to eat and sleep. With both parents working, thousands of children are left to raise themselves.

The structure of the home is different today.

Those who study the future are predicting another change will take place in our homes in the next few years.

First, they are forecasting more and more people will work at home. Millions will do most of their shopping online.

What will life be like in your home? How will things be different? What will remain the same? And how will

this affect your ability to make the home a healthy, nurturing place for your family?

The home used to be a safe sanctuary but today all that has changed. Through television and the Internet excessive violence, sex and a total lack of decency and morals have invaded our homes. What's happening to our society? Why is there an escalating amount of violence, immorality and greed throughout our nation?

What's behind the collapse of our morals? How do you explain corporate executives' dishonesty, leading their companies into bankruptcy to achieve their own gains? Why is it that school violence has exploded?

It seems more people are being driven by hate. Hate groups are publishing their distorted propaganda publicly on their bizarre web pages.

Listen to what one newlywed Gen-Xer said: 'If you flip on the TV you don't see families anymore. Family life is not part of the canon. It takes a lot of faith to reinstate marriage into your vision of life.'

There are many young people who are saying that there are a variety of options and maybe marriage isn't the one for them.

They are saying, 'Living together outside of marriage may be the best option for me.' Without a moral compass, we are thrown into a state of confusion. This is a time of social chaos.

There is cause for concern in the twenty-first century. Is there any north star to guide us? Who shapes our moral values? Where are we heading?

Is morality a matter of personal definition? Is there anything that is secure? Dr Shervert Frazier served as Director of the US National Institute of Mental Health. He expressed concerns in his book *Psycho Trends*. Dr Frazier described what he called 'a co-violent society which celebrates mayhem while simultaneously condemning it'. He says on one hand we condemn violence and on the other hand we feed it to our kids on television.

Set free to obey

On the one hand we condemn murder but on the other we popularise it in our movies.

Something is fundamentally wrong with our society. Our children are exposed to various versions of right and wrong.

There are competing values for the minds of our children. A *Time Magazine* feature article described the US as 'America the Violent'. The article described a nation which feeds on violence and delights in murder in the mass media.

Another article stated that 23,700 people were murdered in US in one year.

Consider this fact about brutality on television. The average 18 year old has witnessed 200,000 violent acts on television and movies, including 40,000 murders.

When you watch 40,000 murders, your mind becomes anaesthetised towards violence. When you see 200,000 violent acts, the message you receive is that violence is an acceptable form of behaviour.

When you fill your mind with immorality, the message is immorality is a perfectly legitimate activity. Our society's motto seems to be, 'If it feels good, do it.' Why is it that we have such high rates of crime? Why is violence so commonplace? Why are marriages breaking up in alarming numbers? The Bible provides some concrete answers.

Here is precisely the problem: Our society has turned its back on God's moral standards. It has cast off God's guidelines.

This society says, 'Your own mind is the standard.' It shouts, 'There is nobody who can tell you what you ought to do.' Solomon emphasises the foolishness of trusting our own mind: 'Those who trust in their own wits are fools' (Proverbs 28:26, NRSV). On their own, our minds can easily deceive us. The Old Testament prophet Isaiah states an eternal truth when he declares, 'All we like sheep have gone astray; we have all turned to our own way' (Isaiah 53:6, NRSV).

You can justify almost anything if you depend on your own thought processes.

We've been sowing the wind of immorality and we've been reaping the whirlwind of divorce.

We've been sowing the wind of explicit sexual content on television and we've been reaping the whirlwind of men with twisted minds preying on our children. There is a cause-and-effect relationship. How do you protect moral values in an immoral world?

We have sown the wind and we are reaping the whirlwind. How can you protect your mind? How can you protect the minds of your children – your grandchildren?

How can you be moral in an immoral world? The book of Revelation provides some clear-cut answers. The book of Revelation is the Revelation of Jesus! It is God's end-time message at the close of Earth's history.

The last book of the Bible, Revelation, has a message for the last generation of men and women living on a planet called Earth.

It is a final message for all humanity, 'Then I saw another angel flying in mid-air, and he had the eternal gospel to proclaim to those who live on the earth – to every nation, tribe, language and people.' (Revelation 14:6.)

Here is an urgent message. Here is a universal message. Here is a message that leaps across geographical boundaries.

Here is a message that penetrates language groups. It is a message that races from north to south, east to west.

It goes to the ends of the earth. What does this message say? Verse 7 says: 'Fear God and give him glory, because the hour of his judgement has come.'

'Fear God' does not mean to be afraid of God. It means reverence, respect and obey God.

But did you notice in this Bible passage the urgency of it all? Let's look at it again. 'Fear God and give him

Set free to obey

glory, *because the hour of his judgement has come.*'

This passage in Revelation answers the question of moral responsibility. Why is there so much crime and violence in society? Why is there so much immorality? Why is there so much lawlessness?

It revolves around the issue of moral responsibility. The judgement calls us to accountability for our actions. The judgement says we are responsible for the choices we make.

When you take the position that you are not responsible to any higher power and that there is no final judgement, there are, in reality, no certain moral standards to guide your life. Judgement implies responsibility and moral choices.

In the last days of earth history, God is calling men and women to judgement. Does God have a standard of morality as a basis for his final judgement? He does. God's law is the basis of morality and the standard of judgement.

The book of Revelation says, you *are* responsible for your actions, 'because the hour of his judgement has come.'

The Bible calls us back to the law of God which is God's eternal moral standard.

The apostle James, the brother of Jesus, puts it this way: 'So speak and so act as those who are to be judged by the law of liberty' (James 2:12, NRSV).

The entire law of God is a law of liberty. Here are a few examples. The sixth commandment: 'You shall not murder' (Exodus 20:13) is liberating. It preserves the sanctity of life. The seventh commandment: 'You shall not commit adultery' (Exodus 20:14) preserves the sanctity of the family. It protects the institution of marriage. The eighth commandment: 'You shall not steal' (Exodus 20:15) is part of this law of liberty.

It protects our possessions and our property.

This is especially true of the Sabbath commandment. The fourth commandment, 'Remember

the Sabbath' liberates us from bondage of work and toil that keeps us enslaved to the world's value system.

The Sabbath, more than any other day, provides parents an opportunity to transmit moral values to their children. It creates an atmosphere for families and friends to recapture spirituality in an age of secularism.

The Sabbath is distinctly designed by God to re-create the Eden experience. God longs for fellowship with his children and as a loving parent anxiously awaits a phone call, a card or email from one of his/her treasured children, so God himself longs for fellowship with us in a taste of eternity each Sabbath.

Notice that God's last-day message for humanity, described as being carried by three angels in mid-heaven, cries with a loud voice, 'Fear God and give him glory, because the hour of his judgement has come. Worship him who made the heavens, the earth, the sea and the springs of water.' (Revelation 14:7.) The Sabbath speaks to us of our loving Creator. Each week we are reminded that we did not evolve. We are sons and daughters of the King. We are not products of chance. Our lives are not a haphazard collection of events over which we have no control. Our personality and character are not solely the products of our heredity and environment. There is a power greater than all of the ugly experiences that have scarred our minds. It is the power of the Creator. The God of Creation can re-create our thought patterns. He can transform our behaviour. He can heal us from within. And this is what the Sabbath is all about. The One who spoke and dry land appeared; the One who spoke and sun, moon and stars were created; this living God can change your life.

The Sabbath speaks of hope. We may be powerless but he is all powerful. We may be weak but he is strong. The Sabbath speaks of a God who wants to write his law on our hearts and minds, just as he did for our first parents in the beginning.

Chapter two
Set free to obey

The Sabbath invites us, as the well-known song says, to 'Turn your eyes upon Jesus, Look full in his wonderful face, And the things of Earth will grow strangely dim, In the light of his glory and grace.'

The law of God sets us free to live an abundant life. Obedience to God's law is Heaven's prescription for joy. Think of the outright chaos in society if the principles of God's law were openly disregarded. If we turned our backs on God's law, our whole society would be turned into mob violence, rampant immorality, pirating, looting and national disaster.

God's law is the foundation of his throne. It is the basis of all law.

But someone says, 'I thought we were saved by grace and we didn't need to keep God's law.' (See Ephesians 2:8.)

When Christ was crucified on the Cross he was judged as a sinner, assuming the guilt of our sins. He was condemned for our sins of which he was not guilty, so we could be pardoned for those very sins of which we are guilty.

If God could have changed his law, Jesus would not have had to die.

The Bible says, 'The wages of sin is death' (Romans 6:23, NRSV).

Why would God send his Son to suffer that cruel death, if all he had to do was to change his law?

Law and judgement are all part of the Gospel of Christ. 'Everyone who commits sin is guilty of lawlessness; sin is lawlessness.' (1 John 3:4, NRSV.)

I may not think it is sin to steal something, but sin is lawlessness. Sin is more than what I think in my own mind. Here is the Bible's definition of sin. Sin is breaking God's law.

A man says, 'Look, I'm not satisfied in my marriage. So if I go out for a weekend with my secretary, it's OK because we're two consenting adults.'

The Bible says, 'You shall not commit adultery.'

When God said REMEMBER

God's law is his eternal moral standard which defines sin and establishes our accountability to God.

And what our children need today is not a diet of murder, violence and immorality on television.

Our children need to be taught the moral principles God has given us.

The moral law of God protects us.

God's law is not some system of regulations to restrict our happiness. God's law is the pathway to freedom and genuine happiness.

God's law protects us from a lifestyle which would destroy us. Some Christians have even said, 'We don't preach on the law in our church. We preach about his love,' as if they are two different things.

Love always leads to obedience. Love doesn't lead to disobedience. It leads committed Christians to keep God's commandments. Jesus said, 'If you love me, you will keep my commandments.' (John 14:15, NRSV.)

Does Jesus say, 'If you love me, you *don't* have to keep my commandments'? No! Love's response is to keep God's commandments.

The reason we obey is not because we are trying to earn God's favour. It's the response of our love for him. I do not obey God to earn my salvation. I obey God, not in order to be saved, but because I am saved.

All my obedience does not earn salvation. Christ wrought that out on the Cross.

But when I come to the Cross my obedience is evidence that I'm saved. First John 2:3 states it clearly:

'We know that we have come to know him if we obey his commands.'

Here, John says, is the evidence that we know God. Here is the evidence that we are born-again believers. Here is the evidence that we are truly Christ's. He who says, 'I know him, but does not do what he commands is a liar, and the truth is not in him.' (1 John 2:4.)

When we are committed to Christ, when we genuinely know him, when our hearts are surrendered

Set free to obey

to him, the natural response is to obey him.

Grace and law are not contradictory ideas. When you are saved by grace you are not saved to disobey. You are saved to obey.

All salvation is by grace. Old Testament believers looked forward to a Christ who was to come. In the New Testament we look to a Christ who has come. They were saved by a grace to come. We are saved by a grace that has come.

But if it's all by grace, what's the role of God's law, then? The apostle Paul makes it plain: '. . . through the law comes the knowledge of sin' (Romans 3:20, NRSV). If you do away with the law, you do away with sin. If there is no law, there is no sin. If there is no sin, there is no need of grace for salvation.

God reveals sin through his law. Paul says: 'If it had not been for the law, I would not have known sin. I would not have known what it is to covet if the law had not said, "You shall not covet." ' (Romans 7:7, NRSV.)

If you break God's law, it is sin. The role of the law is to define sin. The law says, 'This is right and this is wrong.' The law defines the moral standard of God's judgement. The law defines the foundation of all society.

The judgement calls men and women everywhere back to law keeping. It calls Christians who are saved by grace to live obedient, righteous, holy lives.

What is the role of grace?

'For it is by grace you have been saved, through faith – and this not from yourselves, it is the gift of God – not by works, so that no one can boast.' (Ephesians 2:8, 9.) Grace is God's mercy, God's pardon, God's forgiveness. Grace is God's power. Grace is God's love reaching out to sinners. Does grace do away with God's law?

If I am saved by grace, does that lead me to break God's law?

'Do we, then, nullify the law by this faith? Not at all!

Rather, we uphold the law.' (Romans 3:31.)

Paul says, 'Don't think we do away with the law by faith through grace.'

We establish it. We keep it. People who are saved by grace are obedient. Here is a classic example of how grace leads us to keep God's law, not break it.

When you are saved by grace, you are not under the condemnation of the law. Jesus said, 'Do not think that I have come to abolish the Law or the Prophets; I have not come to abolish them but to fulfil them.' (Matthew 5:17.)

Jesus didn't come to do away with the law. Jesus did not come to do away with the fifth commandment which says, 'Honour your father and your mother.' Jesus came to model how a loving son related to his parents. Jesus did not come to do away with the sixth commandment, 'You shall not murder.' He came to reveal kindness and compassion to everyone he came in contact with. Jesus did not come to do away with the seventh commandment, 'You shall not commit adultery.' He came to model purity.

Neither did he come to do away with the fourth commandment, 'Remember the Sabbath day.' This is why the Bible says, 'On the Sabbath day he went into the synagogue, as was his custom.' (Luke 4:16.)

Just as Jesus did not come to abolish the commandments: You shall not steal or murder or commit adultery, or any of the Ten Commandments, he did not come to abolish the Sabbath. The opposite is true. Jesus came to live a life of loving obedience to uphold God's law. The Sabbath commandment is in the heart of the Ten Commandments for a reason. The first four commandments describe our relationship to God. The last four commandments describe our relationship to our fellow man. The Sabbath commandment, calling us to worship our Creator, is the basis for all obedience.

Since he alone is our Creator, we worship him

Set free to obey

exclusively, with no other gods, without images and by not taking his name in vain. Since he is our Creator, we respect every other human being as outlined in the last six commands. The Sabbath commandment explains to us the basis of God's moral authority in giving us the Ten Commandments. He created us. As our Creator he knows what's best. The Ten Commandments are guidelines for living from a caring Creator, and honouring him on the Sabbath as Creator is the foundation for that obedience.

According to the apostle Paul, 'God . . . created all things through Jesus Christ' (Ephesians 3:9, NKJV). As Creator, Jesus kept the Sabbath in honour of the Father's plan and as a model of true Sabbath worship.

Confusion over law and grace

Most Christians are confused about the relationship between law and grace. The apostle Paul declared, 'For sin shall not be your master, because you are not under law, but under grace.' (Romans 6:14.)

When does sin have dominion over you? When you follow your way, rather than God's way. When you break God's law, sin enslaves you.

What does it mean to be under the law? To be under the law means to be under the law as a means of salvation. Attempting to keep the law in our own strength is like attempting to swim across the Atlantic Ocean. You may be an Olympic world-class swimmer but the distance is just too far. No matter how hard we try, it is impossible to keep God's law on our own. If we look to our law keeping as a means of salvation we will be constantly frustrated in our futile attempts to obey. We will feel continually condemned. But if Jesus is our source of salvation, everything changes.

To be under grace means that I accept Christ's pardon, receive Christ's forgiveness and am filled with his power.

Christ writes his law in my heart and in my mind. I

desire to obey him.

The Bible is very clear on this subject. When we
come to Jesus Christ and cast ourselves upon his
mercy, he says, 'My child, no matter what you have
done in the past, no matter how sinful your life has
been, my child, I will forgive you. You can begin again.'
The law reveals our need.

When I look at God's law, I see who I am. I don't
measure up to God's moral standards.

I see times when I have been impatient. I see times
when I haven't been as kind as I should have been. My
failure to keep God's law leads me to seek God's
grace. This is what the psalmist David meant when he
declared, 'The law of the LORD is perfect, converting
the soul' (Psalms 19:7, NKJV). The ten commandment
law drives me to Jesus, and I say, 'Oh, Jesus, my heart
is broken. I am crushed because of my sin. Jesus,
forgive me. Take away my guilt. Lead me, dear Jesus,
to keep your law. Help me to be obedient.'

There was a time when a lawyer came to Jesus and
asked, 'Teacher, which is the greatest commandment in
the Law? Jesus replied: "Love the Lord your God with
all your heart and with all your soul and with all your
mind." This is the first and greatest commandment.
And the second is like it: "Love your neighbour as
yourself." ' (Matthew 22:36-39.)

What was Jesus doing? He was summarising the
Ten Commandments. Jesus further explained this way:
'All the Law and the Prophets hang on these two
commandments.' (vs 40.)

The entire law can be summarised in one word –
love.

Jesus summarised the first four commandments
with *love* to God and the last six commandments with
love to our fellow man.

Jesus was saying: If you love fully, you will love God.
If you love fully, you will love your fellow man.

Love always leads to obedience.

Chapter two
Set free to obey

God's ten commandment law was written with his finger on tables of stone.

Keeping God's law doesn't put you in bondage; it takes you out of bondage.

The Ten Commandments were not given to restrict our freedom. They were given so we could be truly free.

They were given by God himself. Listen to how they are introduced: 'I am the LORD your God . . .' (Exodus 20:2, NKJV). It is the Lord God, the Lord of Heaven and Earth, who wrote these commandments with his own finger on tables of stone as moral principles for all time.

Let's review the Ten Commandments – God's moral guidelines for living.

'You shall have no other gods before me.' (Exodus 20:3.)

God is saying, 'I must be supreme in your life.' No other gods, not your house, not money, not tobacco, not materialism – nothing else will satisfy.

The second commandment states, 'You shall not make for yourself an idol . . .' (vs 4).

In other words, worship God supremely. God says, 'Don't come to me through images. Come to me directly.'

The third commandment declares, 'You shall not misuse the name of the LORD your God.' (vs 7.)

God is saying, 'Love me enough to respect my name.'

Think of it, the name of Jesus. The name at which angels veil their faces is being dragged through the dust with vile curses.

The ten commandment law speaks with relevance to our time, urging us to use Jesus' name reverently, only in ways which bring honour to him.

The fourth commandment regarding the Sabbath is in the heart of God's law. God commanded all mankind to remember, but it seems that most have forgotten.

'Remember the Sabbath day, to keep it holy. Six

days you shall labour and do all your work, but the seventh day is the Sabbath of the LORD your God.' (Exodus 20:8-10, NKJV.)

In an age of godless evolution God calls us to worship the Creator of Heaven and Earth. The Sabbath command liberates us from the tyranny of the earthly and puts us in touch with eternal values each week. It frees us from our mind-numbing attachment to things and puts us in contact with divine realities.

The fifth commandment, 'Honour your father and your mother' has a promise to go along with it: 'so that you may live long in the land the LORD your God is giving you.' (vs 12.)

What a promise! There is a relationship between health, long life, happiness and positive relationships between parents and their children.

The sixth commandment speaks with relevance: 'You shall not murder.' (vs 13.)

At a time when military arsenals are being built to kill millions; at a time when snipers destroy innocent lives; there is still a commandment that says life is sacred: 'You shall not murder.' The sixth commandment liberates all people to be free from killing, murder and war. It calls upon all to recognise that life is a gift that comes from God.

The seventh commandment shouts to this generation, 'You shall not commit adultery.' (vs 14.)

At a time of immorality, at a time when there is a lack of moral purity, God's law speaks to this generation.

When a society turns its back on God's law, when it is openly immoral, that society is on its way to disaster. The seventh commandment is a call to moral purity. It frees us from the sexually transmitted diseases which are devastating entire countries. It calls us from the physical, mental and emotional brokenness of disregarding the laws of purity written in the fabric of our being. It frees us from the horrible guilt resulting from breaking this basic law of morality.

Set free to obey

The eighth commandment, 'You shall not steal' (vs 15), protects the possessions God has graciously given us. It's still wrong to steal. It's still wrong to shoplift. It's still wrong to take something that does not belong to you. The eighth commandment frees us to be secure in what we have without the fear of someone else selfishly taking it away.

The ninth commandment, 'You shall not give false testimony against your neighbour' (vs 16), protects our reputations. Lying is still wrong. Gossip is still wrong. Dragging someone's good name through the dust is still wrong.

Our reputations and good names are protected by God.

The tenth commandment is God's appeal for us to be content. It is Heaven's call for us to rest in his goodness. The final command, 'You shall not covet' (vs 17), focuses on minds praising God for the good things he gives us, rather than complaining about what we do not have.

The ten commandment law speaks to this generation. The ten commandment law speaks with meaning to our society today.

Satan lost Heaven because of disobedience.

Adam and Eve lost Eden because of disobedience.

God is calling his people back to his ten commandment law.

He gives us this promise:

'This is the covenant that I will make with the house of Israel after those days, says the LORD: I will put my laws in their minds and write them on their hearts, and I will be their God, and they shall be my people.' (Hebrews 8:10, NRSV.)

God says, 'I am going to put my law in your mind.' What does this mean? If God's law is in our minds, we know it. If God's law is in our hearts, we love it. God will have a last-day people who have his commandments written in their hearts and minds.

They love him enough to obey him. Through God's grace they are set free to obey. They are liberated through the power of Christ from evil's grasp. They are delivered from its bondage. In Jesus they are free – free to live godly, obedient lives. Notice the following description of this last-day people.

'Here is the patience of the saints; here are those who keep the commandments of God and the faith of Jesus.' (Revelation 14:12, NKJV.)

Here they are. The faithful ones – those who keep the commandments of God and have the faith of Jesus. The last chapter in Revelation describes the redeemed this way:

'Blessed are those who do his commandments, that they may have the right to the tree of life, and may enter through the gates into the city.' (Revelation 22:14, NKJV.)

Jesus Christ pardons us. Jesus says, 'Come to me, my child.' He gives us mercy. Christ looks into our eyes and says, 'I have something special I want to do for you. I want to change your life. I would like to make you a new man or a new woman.'

Would you like to say, 'Jesus, come into my life. Jesus, do for me what it is impossible for me to do for myself'?

Is there anything more important to you than reaching out and taking Jesus' hand right now? His grace will pardon your past. His grace will transform your life. His grace will make you a new man or a new woman.

I love that old hymn, 'Marvellous grace of our loving Lord, Grace that exceeds our sin and our guilt! Yonder on Calvary's mount outpoured, There where the blood of the Lamb was spilled. Grace, grace, God's grace, Grace that will pardon and cleanse within; Grace, grace, God's grace, Grace that is greater than all our sin. Marvellous, infinite, matchless grace, Freely bestowed on all who believe . . .'

Chapter two
Set free to obey

His grace flows from his throne to your heart right now. Why not commit your life to him right now? Why not open your heart to his grace which will pardon you from your past guilt and lead you to live an obedient life?

Why not tell him in the quietness of your soul that you want to humbly obey him? Why not thank him that his way is truly best – that obeying him is truly your delight?

——— Chapter three ———

A day to remember

In 1991 the COBE satellite produced what some scientists called the discovery of the century. Those letters, COBE, represented the Cosmic Background Explorer. You may remember reading about the amazing launch of the COBE satellite. Astronomers, astrophysicists and cosmologists were astounded.

When it comes to the question of the origin of life, there are only two possible positions. Either matter always existed or God always existed. The evolutionist says that matter always existed. The COBE satellite indicated from the data regarding the universe that the universe had a definite beginning.

When the COBE satellite measured the limitless realms of space, studying the great origins of life, its measurements sent shockwaves through the scientific world. They indicated that matter did not always exist. COBE data regarding the universe indicated that it had a definite beginning.

Dr Hugh Ross wrote about this unusual discovery in his book, *The Creator and the Cosmos*. He asserts one of the greatest discoveries of the century reveals that there is a God. Dr Ross put it this way: 'The measured proportion exactly fit the proportion you would expect – if the universe had a beginning. That's what the COBE satellite told us.'

Previously, when scientists considered the universe, they believed matter was infinite – that it never had a beginning – but the evidence from COBE challenged

A day to remember

this assumption.

Could it be that if there was a beginning then there was a *Beginner*; if there was a creation then there was a *Creator*?

Science is taking another look. A Berkley astronomer, speaking about the COBE satellite, said: 'What we have found is evidence of the birth of the universe. . . . It's like looking at God.'

God's fingerprints

In the marvels of Creation, God has left his fingerprints throughout the universe. There are scientists who, observing God's Creation, see his handiwork. They see evidence for his existence. They see evidence for a Creator God – one who fashioned the world.

The Bible's last book, Revelation, describes a clarion call for men and women living in Earth's last hour to return to this Creator God. In prophetic vision, the apostle John saw the throne room of the universe.

His angelic visitor invited him into the presence of God. The angel said, 'Come up here, and I will show you what must take place after this.' (Revelation 4:1.)

In prophetic vision John travelled to the throne room of the universe. He saw heavenly beings singing songs of praise. 'Holy, holy, holy is the Lord God Almighty, who was, and is, and is to come.' (Revelation 4:8.)

'You are worthy, our Lord and God, to receive glory and honour and power, for you created all things, and by your will they were created and have their being.' (Revelation 4:11.)

All of Heaven sings. Some scientists may question. Some intellectuals may doubt. Some academics may wonder. Yet all of Heaven sings, 'You are worthy, our Lord and God, to receive glory and honour and power.' Why? Because 'you created all things, and by your will they were created and have their being.' We do not exist by mere chance. We are not some accidental

combination of molecules. We are not some random combination of genes and chromosomes.

We were created by a loving God. Before you existed in the womb of your mother, you existed in the mind of God.

God fashioned you. God shaped you. God created you. The book of Revelation calls humanity back to worshipping the Creator.

The book of Revelation declares, 'Praise and glory and wisdom and thanks and honour and power and strength be to our God for ever and ever.' (Revelation 7:12.) It calls us to worship 'him who lives for ever and ever, who created the heavens and all that is in them, the earth and all that is in it, and the sea and all that is in it,' (Revelation 10:6). In Revelation 10, an angel comes down from Heaven. He puts one foot on the land and one foot on the sea, indicating a universal message for all peoples, and cries out, 'Worship the Creator.'

Why is it that God is worthy of worship?

God is worthy of our praise because he made us. He fashioned us. He created us. We did not evolve.

God is worthy of worship because he has given us life. And we respond to this marvellous gift of life by giving him worship and praise and honour.

How did we lose this concept of God as our Creator? What events led up to modern science's dismissal of the concept of God as maker of the heavens and the earth? Was there a 'tipping point' – a point in time when things began to change?

Charles Darwin

In 1831 a young scientist, Charles Darwin, made an epic journey to the Galapagos Islands on the *Beagle*. There Darwin studied what seemed to be the almost endless variety of birds, reptiles and sea life. He was fascinated with the species of flora and fauna found on the island. He noted, for example, that turtles and

A day to remember

lizards and finches showed a great variety within the same species. Since the popular teaching of the Church at this time was that God created every species we currently see, and he observed evolution within the species, Darwin cast off what he believed was the archaic, unscientific notion of the Church and accepted a radically different view.

He believed that the variety he saw in nature was an indication that the species evolved. Although Darwin saw gaps between kinds of plants and animals, he assumed future generations of scientists would discover the link between these kinds. Darwin's major assumption that links between the kinds existed was flawed.

Darwin taught that natural law explained the reason for our existence. He ruled an all-powerful Creator out of the picture. Darwin's book, *The Origin of Species*, transformed the way millions looked at the world. His new world had no place for a Creator. In Darwin's view, human beings evolved over millions of years from the lower to the higher forms of life. And to think, millions of minds were changed based on an assumption – an unproven idea – that there are clear links between species!

Now people around the world have accepted this teaching of evolution. Although there is evidence in the natural world of infinite variety between the species, Darwin's theory of evolution did not answer all the questions about the origin of life. There are still huge gaps and big questions. Here are just a few of them.

1. If evolution is true, where are the gaps between the species? How do we fill in the missing links? Where is the missing link between a variety of animal species? Between humans and animals? Between sea creatures and land creatures and so on?

2. It is a law of biology that says life produces life. Darwin says, given enough time, non-living things will produce living things, yet there is no evidence of

this in the scientific world. Why?

3. It is a law of biology that says like produces like; randomness tends to break down, not restore. Evolution says things which are not alike can ultimately be produced from things which are alike. In other words, one species can produce another species totally distinct from the first species.

But God has an answer to the problem of evolution. It is part of his final message for all people.

Judgement

Revelation calls us to 'Fear God and give him glory, because the hour of his judgment has come. Worship him who made the heavens, the earth, the sea and the springs of water.' (Revelation 14:7.)

This is a message for all of us. It's not a message of one religious group or another.

It is God's final call to all his people. It is a call to worship the Creator. How do we worship the Creator of Heaven and Earth?

How does he remind us of his re-creative power? At Creation did he leave us a symbol of his creative authority? Revelation is the book of endings. We can only understand the book of endings if we understand the book of beginnings. We will only understand the significance of the monumental issues in today's world if we understand the events at Creation. Revelation's final call for the entire human race to worship the Creator has its origin in Genesis – the book of beginnings.

This theme of true worship – remembering the Creator – is a common thread throughout the Bible. It is one of the most important themes of Scripture.

The heart of Revelation's final crisis is over true and false worship. Worshipping the Creator is at the centre of it all. Let's return to our origin so we can understand our destiny. Let's return to the book of beginnings, Genesis, so we can understand the book of endings,

A day to remember

Revelation. The amazingly intricate world as we know it today was created in six literal days.

God spoke this dark, shapeless mass into existence. He dazzled it with light, enveloped it with atmosphere, brightened it with babbling brooks and flowing rivers, coloured it with beautiful flowers and plants, enlivened it with an incredible variety of living things, and looked upon his handiwork and said, 'It is good!'

And then came the crowning act of Creation. 'Let us make man in our image . . . in the image of God he created him; male and female he created them.' (Genesis 1:26, 27.)

Human beings could receive no greater honour! God could have shown no greater love! The human race is God's masterpiece of Creation – the object of his supreme love! This love was meant to be shared, for God said: 'Be fruitful and increase in number; fill the earth and subdue it. Rule over . . . every living creature . . .' (Genesis 1:28). After the creation of Adam and Eve on the sixth day, the Bible says: 'Thus the heavens and the earth were completed in all their vast array.' (Genesis 2:1.)

Just six days of work and Creation was done. Such a short time! But not for God! The Bible says: 'For he spoke, and it came to be; he commanded, and it stood firm.' (Psalms 33:9, NRSV.) Adam and Eve must have gazed in wide-eyed wonder as the blazing sun, in all its glory, began to slip beneath the western horizon, ending the sixth day of Creation.

But the Genesis account of Creation does not end there. The Bible record continues: 'By the seventh day God had finished the work he had been doing; so on the seventh day he rested from all his work.' (Genesis 2:2.)

God rested! Why? Not because he was weary. The prophet Isaiah tells us that God never gets weary (see Isaiah 40:28). The Creator of the universe permitted himself the satisfaction of enjoying his completed

Creation.

God was pleased with his accomplishments over Earth's first six days. Then God did something especially significant. 'God blessed the seventh day and made it holy, because on it he rested from all the work of creating that he had done.' (Genesis 2:3.)

The seventh day Sabbath, given at Creation, was to be God's perpetual reminder of our roots.

The Bible says, 'God blessed the seventh day.' He made the seventh day an endless fountain of spiritual refreshing for his people for all time to come.

Next, he sanctified the seventh day! He set it apart as a holy day, a special time every seven days continually to remind us of our beginnings – our origin! Here are three specific things God did on the seventh day.

1. God blessed it.
2. God sanctified it.
3. God rested on it.

The Bible does *not* say that God blessed the first day or the third day or the fifth day or any other day except the seventh.

And what God blesses, according to 1 Chronicles 17:27, he blesses forever. To bless is to infuse something with God's very presence. God blessed the seventh day by making it an eternal sign of his powerful Creation and infinite love. Each Sabbath as we worship the Creator of the universe, we, too, will receive God's special blessing – the blessing of his peace, the blessing of his presence, the blessing of his renewed strength and the blessing of his eternal perspective of life's true meaning. The blessing of Sabbath is the blessing of a joy-filled heart worshipping the God who made us.

He rested on the seventh day, not because *he* was tired, but because he knew *we* would be tired. God sanctified the seventh day. He set it apart for holy use.

A day to remember

A universal Sabbath

The Sabbath was created by God more than two thousand years before the existence of the Jewish race. The nation of Israel traces its origin back to Abraham. Abraham's son, Isaac, through Sarah in their old age became the child of promise. Isaac's son, Jacob, had twelve sons whose families were the origin of the twelve tribes of Israel. Abraham, Isaac and Jacob lived well over two millenniums after Creation. Over 100,000 Sabbaths were already kept by the people of God before the existence of the Jewish nation. The Sabbath was given at Creation for all peoples as a day to worship the Creator and praise him for the gift of life itself. This is precisely why Jesus said, 'The Sabbath was made for man, not man for the Sabbath.' (Mark 2:27.) God created the Sabbath to be a blessing to all humanity. This is why he blessed it at Creation. This is why he set it aside and sanctified it at Creation. This is why he left us the gift of his rest at Creation.

The Sabbath was given to our parents, Adam and Eve, in the Garden of Eden. The Sabbath was set aside at Creation as an eternal symbol of God's creative power for his people in every age. When Adam and Eve left the garden, the Sabbath remained as a reminder of God's eternal love. Throughout both the Old and New Testaments the Sabbath is a sign between God and his people. Before he gave the Israelites the ten commandment law on Mount Sinai, they were keeping the Sabbath of Creation. In Exodus 16, we read the remarkable story of the falling of the manna.

The Lord said: 'Six days you are to gather it, but on the seventh day, the Sabbath, there will not be any.' (Exodus 16:26.) God worked a miracle for Israel. He met their needs by raining bread down from Heaven. This bread or manna fell every day except on Sabbath.

If the Israelites gathered more than they could eat, the leftover portion spoiled. In addition, twice as much

manna fell on Friday. The Israelites then gathered a double portion which God miraculously preserved over the Sabbath. This Sabbath miracle during the years of wilderness wandering kept the Israelites constantly aware of the fact that they belonged to God. When some Israelites went out to gather manna on the Sabbath, God said: 'How long will you refuse to keep my commands and my instructions?' (Exodus 16:28.)

Even before God gave the Ten Commandments in written form on Mount Sinai his people knew his commands. It was wrong for Cain to kill Abel even before the Ten Commandments were given at Sinai. Abraham kept God's ten commandment law before Sinai (Genesis 26:5). The Israelites wandering in the wilderness kept the Sabbath before Mount Sinai.

When God created Adam and Eve he wrote his commandments in their hearts and minds. For example, Cain knew it was wrong to murder Abel. The Israelites knew it was wrong to break the Sabbath. The Ten Commandments were given on Mount Sinai, not because God's people did not know right from wrong from the beginning, but because in their sinfulness and rebellion they needed God's law restored.

On Mount Sinai God wrote the Ten Commandments on tables of stone. He didn't write these commandments on the sand to be washed away. He did not write them on parchment to be consumed by fire. God did not write the Sabbath command on a little piece of paper hidden in a corner. God wrote on tables of stone. God wrote the law to endure forever. God didn't even entrust Moses to write it. God didn't entrust one of the prophets to write it. If in the Bible there is only one set of laws written with God's own finger, if God wrote them on tables of stone, can we turn our backs on the eternal law of God lightly? The Bible says: 'Remember the Sabbath day, to keep it holy' (Exodus 20:8, NKJV).

Chapter three
A day to remember

Why 'Remember'?

We can keep holy only what God has made holy. Human beings can't make something holy. God made the Sabbath holy. He blessed it at Creation. He says: *Remember*. Why did God say remember? He knew we would forget. He knew in this secular, materialistic age men and women would forget the Sabbath. So God said, 'Remember the Sabbath day, to keep it holy.' God is calling us back to his eternal sign of Creation. It unites us with him. 'Remember the Sabbath day, to keep it holy. Six days you shall labour and do all your work, but the seventh day is the Sabbath of the LORD your God. In it you shall do no work . . .' (Exodus 20:9, 10 [first part], NKJV).

Does the Sabbath command say, 'It's the Sabbath of the Jew'? No. It says it's 'the Sabbath of the LORD your God.' Why is the seventh-day Sabbath the Sabbath of the Lord your God?

The origin of the Sabbath is not some bishop or priest or pastor. It is not some church council. The origin of the Sabbath is the Creator himself. It is his sign. It is his memorial. It is his emblem. It is his command. As a bulwark against evolution, he fashioned it to call us to worship him as Creator of Heaven and Earth. In keeping the Sabbath we acknowledge that every heartbeat comes from him. We declare every breath comes from him.

As we rest and worship him on the Sabbath, we are declaring allegiance to him as our Creator. We declare, 'God, we did not create our own life. You are the giver of life.' He does not say, *a* seventh day is the Sabbath. He says *the* seventh day is the Sabbath. And just as all the celebrations of the day before your birthday or the day after your birthday do not establish those days as your birthday, so all the celebrations the day before or the day after do not make those days the true Bible Sabbath. You can have a birthday party the day before or the day after your birthday, but that does not change

the day you were born. Celebrating the Sabbath on the sixth day or the first day does not change the reality of the fact that God set aside the seventh-day Sabbath. He commanded, 'Remember the Sabbath day.' But millions have forgotten to remember. For them the Sabbath is no more than a common, ordinary day. What day did God bless? The seventh day. What day did God sanctify? The seventh day. What day did God rest on? The seventh day.

In the heart of the ten commandment law, God tells us why we are to worship on the Sabbath. 'For in six days the LORD made the heavens and the earth, the sea, and all that is in them, and rested the seventh day. Therefore the LORD blessed the Sabbath day and hallowed it.' (Exodus 20:11, NKJV.)

The ten commandment law quotes Genesis and leads us back to the time God created the earth. The Sabbath was never an exclusively Jewish institution. It was given for all of us. The Ten Commandments are God's unchangeable laws for all humanity. The commandment 'You shall not commit adultery' is not only for the Jews. The commandment 'You shall not murder' is not only for the Jews. The commandment 'You shall not make for yourself an idol' is not only for the Jews. The Sabbath is not exclusively a Jewish Sabbath. These commands reveal the best way to live. They are the foundation for a happy, productive, meaningful life.

The Sabbath command is not for some of us, it is for all of us. The prophet Isaiah says, 'All who keep the sabbath, and do not profane it . . . I will bring to my holy mountain, and make them joyful in my house of prayer; . . . for my house shall be called a house of prayer for all peoples.' (Isaiah 56:6, 7, NRSV.) God says, 'All nations will one day worship around my throne in the New Jerusalem each Sabbath.' This is the vision of God's house of prayer we saw in the book of Revelation. It's the New Jerusalem. It's there at God's

A day to remember

throne where all of God's people are singing praise to the Creator. The seventh-day Sabbath – the day God rested on, the day God sanctified, the day God blessed – is the golden link that links the Creation in Genesis with the new creation in the book of Revelation.

The eternal principles of God's law are universal and so is the Sabbath. It was never done away with. It was never changed. It was written on tables of stone with God's own finger. Throughout the Old Testament the Sabbath was God's everlasting sign for all his people. The prophet Ezekiel clarifies the eternal nature of the Sabbath in these words, 'Moreover I gave them my sabbaths, as a sign between me and them, so that they might know that I the LORD sanctify them.' (Ezekiel 20:12, NRSV.)

The Sabbath is not only a sign that God created us, it is a sign that he can re-create our hearts. The Sabbath is a symbol of sanctification. The word *sanctification* simply means *to be made holy*. Just as we did not create ourselves, we cannot re-create ourselves. We cannot make ourselves holy. Only God can make us holy through his Holy Spirit. The Sabbath is a symbol of the God whose power made the world and the God whose power can remake our hearts.

Jesus and the Sabbath

God gave the Sabbath to Adam and Eve at Creation. God gave the Sabbath to Moses in the ten commandment law at Sinai. He gave the Sabbath as a sign of his creative authority, eternal power and everlasting love throughout the Old Testament.

The questions are often raised, 'What about the New Testament? What about Jesus Christ?' Did Jesus come to do away with the Sabbath? Did the disciples change the Sabbath? Did they worship on another day? Let's look at the New Testament. What did Jesus teach about the Bible Sabbath?

'He went to Nazareth, where he had been brought

up, and on the Sabbath day he went into the synagogue, as was his custom. And he stood up to read.' (Luke 4:16.) Jesus had a custom or practice. Each Sabbath the Saviour found joy in worship.

If Jesus wanted to leave another sign or symbol of worship, wouldn't we expect him to leave us a positive example in his life? Isn't it true that a person's will and testament is sealed by his or her death? You cannot change a man's will after he dies. And Christ's will and testament was sealed at his death. The legacy of his life was a positive example of Sabbath keeping. Christ kept the Bible Sabbath.

The Sabbath was made for Jews and Gentiles alike as a sign of true worship. It is a sign that we worship him exclusively. It is a sign that we love him supremely.

We were not made for the Sabbath. The Sabbath was made as God's gift to us. Adam and Eve were made first. The Sabbath is God's love gift to the human race. Every Sabbath we flee from the stresses of life to his palace in time. The tensions of life evaporate in his presence. The Sabbath is an eternal sign that he created us. We rest in a completed Creation. And we rest in a completed redemption.

In life and in death Jesus rested on the Bible Sabbath. The Sabbath was written on tables of stone, never to be changed – never to be altered.

Jesus never placed any doubt regarding what day the Sabbath was. He did question all the legalistic requirements the Jews piled up on the Sabbath. That's why Jesus said, 'It is lawful to do good on the Sabbath.' (Matthew 12:12.) For Christ, the Sabbath was a day for works of mercy – a wonderful day of worship and praise, a day of fellowship, blessing and healing. Jesus performed more miracles on the Sabbath than on any other day. Although he was severely criticised as a Sabbath breaker, Jesus established the Sabbath as a day of blessing and doing good to others.

The Sabbath was not some legalistic, narrow-minded requirement. Even in death Jesus Christ kept the Sabbath. Jesus' closest followers rested according to the commandment on the seventh-day Sabbath.

They wouldn't even embalm his body on Sabbath. Jesus rested on Sabbath before he was resurrected on the first day of the week. Jesus kept the Sabbath in life and Jesus kept the Sabbath in death.

Love leads us to obedience. Love leads us to keep his commandments. When I kneel at the foot of the Cross and I see those nails driven through his hands, I long to obey him.

At the Cross there is mercy. At the Cross there is forgiveness. At the Cross our hearts are changed. We kneel there in wonder and amazement that he could love us so. We hear him say, 'If you love me, you will obey what I command.' (John 14:15.) Obedience is not a duty; it is a delight. Love prompts us to worship him every Sabbath. We are not driven by some legalistic requirement. We are driven by love.

We give our lives back to the one who gave his life for us. Jesus did not view the Sabbath as a 'Jewish custom' to be kept temporarily until his death on the Cross. He did not teach that the Sabbath was limited to Hebrews in the first century. For Jesus, the Sabbath was an eternal symbol of his creative power; keeping the Sabbath reveals an inner sense of loyalty to him.

On one occasion Jesus met with his closest followers and revealed that even after his crucifixion, death and resurrection, the Sabbath would be kept. In a carefully crafted sermon, he discussed the coming destruction of Jerusalem. He instructed his disciples, 'And pray that your flight will not take place in winter or on the Sabbath.' (Matthew 24:20.)

What sense would it make for Jesus to say to his disciples, 'Pray that your flight will not take place on the Sabbath,' if they were not going to be keeping the Sabbath? It wouldn't have made any sense at all.

If Christians had all been worshipping on the

Sabbath together in one Jerusalem location, and the Roman armies had attacked the city, what would have happened? It would have been much easier for the Roman armies to destroy them all. The historian Josephus tells us that the Roman armies actually approached Jerusalem on the Sabbath.

Jesus said, 'Pray that your flight will not take place on the Sabbath.' These first-century Christians did pray. Miraculously, the Roman armies pulled back for apparently no reason. This gave the Christians a brief moment of time to escape from the city. As a result, there is not a single record of any Christians being destroyed during the destruction of Jerusalem.

Jerusalem was destroyed in AD70, years after Jesus had long since ascended to Heaven.

Has the calendar been changed?

How can we really know which day the Sabbath is? Is the seventh day of the week today the same as the seventh day of Bible times? Hasn't the calendar been changed?

There are at least three ways you can know. You can know from the Bible; you can know from language; you can know from astronomy. You will recall that the Sabbath was stated at Creation and it was re-stated in the Ten Commandments given to Moses. It is clear there was no time lost between Adam and Moses. Adam kept the seventh-day Sabbath and so did Moses. All through the Old Testament, from Moses to Jesus, God's people kept the Sabbath, so there was no time lost there. The crucifixion story clearly reveals that the weekly cycle as we know it has not changed from Jesus' time until today.

Let's look at this sequence of days from the Bible. We begin with the day Jesus died. The Bible describes it this way: 'It was Preparation Day, and the Sabbath was about to begin. The women who had come with Jesus from Galilee followed Joseph and saw the tomb

A day to remember

and how his body was laid in it. Then they went home and prepared spices and perfumes. But they rested on the Sabbath in obedience to the commandment.' (Luke 23:54-56.)

Were the closest followers of Jesus keeping the Sabbath after he died? What does Luke's account say? 'But they rested on the Sabbath in obedience to the commandment' (verse 56). They did not believe that his death changed the commandment in any way.

Here we have three days listed in succession. First, the day he died. Second, the day he rested in the tomb. Third, the first day of the week, the day he rose from the dead. Then the Bible says, 'On the first day of the week, very early in the morning, the women took the spices they had prepared and went to the tomb.' (Luke 24:1.)

Let's consider the order of events occurring on these three days carefully. The Preparation day, the day Christ died, is commonly celebrated as Good Friday. This is followed by the seventh-day Sabbath. On Sabbath, Christ's closest followers rested according to the commandment. Jesus, the divine Son of God, also rested in the tomb on Sabbath.

Jesus was resurrected from the dead on the first day of the week – the day millions of Christians celebrate as Easter Sunday. The identity of the seventh-day Sabbath is clear. It is the day between the day Jesus died (Friday) and the day he arose (Sunday) – the day we call Saturday. It may seem a bit surprising to discover Saturday is the true Bible Sabbath.

There are eight texts in the New Testament that mention the first day of the week, and not one of them tells us to worship on Sunday in honour of the resurrection. Christ has given us a symbol of the resurrection. How do we celebrate the resurrection? Let's allow the Bible to speak for itself. 'Or don't you know that all of us who were baptised into Christ Jesus were baptised into his death? We were therefore buried

with him through baptism into death in order that, just as Christ was raised from the dead through the glory of the Father, we too may live a new life.' (Romans 6:3, 4.)

Baptism is the New Testament symbol of the resurrection. As new believers enter into the baptismal pool, they are fully immersed, signifying death to the old life. Coming up out of the water, they are resurrected to live a new life in Jesus.

Just as Jesus entered the grave and arose to new life, so baptism symbolises the new life given to each born-again Christian through the power of the Holy Spirit. Baptism is the symbol of resurrection power, not Sunday observance.

The Bible says, 'Remember the Sabbath day.' We honour him as Creator by keeping the Bible Sabbath. In over 140 languages of the world, the word for the seventh day of the week is Sabbath.

In Russian, Ukrainian and Bulgarian, it is *Sabbota*. In Arabic it is *As-Sabat*. In Hebrew it is *Shabbat*. The languages of the world make it very plain – the day we call Saturday in English is called Sabbath. According to such trustworthy sources as the Greenwich Observatory and the United States Naval Observatory, the weekly cycle has never changed. History does tell us that in AD1582 Pope Gregory XIII changed the date to adjust for the calendar drifting from the actual seasons.

He decreed that the day following Thursday 4 October 1582 would be Friday 15 October 1582.

But note that this change did not disturb the weekly cycle. Friday still followed Thursday, and Saturday followed Friday. And Sunday was still the first day of the week. Decades ago in 1976, I wrote to the Astronomer Royal at the Greenwich Observatory for information regarding the unbroken sequence of the weekly cycle. I wanted to be absolutely sure there was no evidence of any change. Here is my letter and please notice carefully the information officer's reply.

A day to remember

Dear Sir,
I am currently doing research regarding the unbroken sequence of
the weekly cycle. Various European astronomers state that the
weekly cycle has come down to us unbroken from ancient times. In
other words, that the seventh day of our present week, for example,
is identical with the seventh day of the week of Bible times.
My question is threefold.

1) What does your investigation show regarding the unbroken
antiquity of the weekly cycle from ancient times?
2) Have other changes in the calendar in past centuries (Julian to
Gregorian, and so on) affected, in any way, the cycle of the week?
3) Is the Saturday of our present time the lineal descent in unbroken
cycles of seven from that Saturday mentioned in the Bible record
of the crucifixion?

I greatly appreciate your time in answering these questions and
look forward to your soon reply.
Sincerely,
Mark Finley

Reply from R. H. Tucker, Information Officer, Royal
Greenwich Observatory, 1976.

Dear Sir,
Your letter to the Astronomer Royal at
Greenwich has been sent on to us here and the
Director has asked me to reply.

The continuity of the seven-day week has been
maintained since the earliest days of the Jewish
religion. The astronomer may be concerned in the
decisions relating to the time, the calendar date,
and the year number. But since the week is a civil,
social, and religious cycle, there should be no
reason why it should be disturbed by any
adjustment to the calendar. Any attempt to disturb
the seven-day cycle has always aroused the most
determined opposition of the Jewish authorities,

and we are quite certain that no such disturbance
has ever been put into effect. The change from the
Julian to Gregorian calendar (1582-1927) has
always been made to leave the weekday sequence
undisturbed.

Yours faithfully,

R. H. Tucker

Information Officer

The Sabbath of the disciples

If you still have any doubt, simply consult *Webster's International Dictionary* for Saturday. You will read, 'Saturday is the seventh day of the week.' Adam kept the Sabbath. Moses kept the Sabbath. Isaiah kept the Sabbath. Jeremiah kept the Sabbath. *Jesus* kept the Sabbath. Peter, James, John and Paul kept the Sabbath. The New Testament makes the Sabbath practices of the disciples plain.

'They came to Thessalonica, where there was a Jewish synagogue. As his custom was, Paul went into the synagogue, and on three Sabbath days he reasoned with them from the Scriptures.' (Acts 17:1, 2.)

Paul preached about Christ. It was the Sabbath. The interesting thing is that Gentiles regularly attended these Sabbath meetings as well. Luke records in Acts 13:42, 'The people urged them to speak about these things again the next sabbath.' (NRSV.) The apostle Paul did not encourage them to return on the first day to keep Sunday. The scripture says, 'The next sabbath almost the whole city gathered to hear the word of the Lord.' (Acts 13:44, NRSV.)

A whole city is coming! Praise God! What if everyone in your city came to worship the Creator every Sabbath? The Sabbath reveals a oneness or unity between all peoples. In Christ we are part of a common creation forged together as one human race. And on the Sabbath we celebrate our oneness.

When we come to worship him on Sabbath he

A day to remember

bonds us together as one humanity. The disciples kept the Sabbath both in public, and when there was no common gathering of believers, they kept the Sabbath with a small group privately.

'On the Sabbath we went outside the city gate to the river, where we expected to find a place of prayer. We sat down and began to speak to the women who had gathered there.' (Acts 16:13.)

In this city, there was no Sabbath-keeping group or church. So the apostle Paul met with a group of believers by a quiet river to worship on the Sabbath.

The New Testament evidence is plain. He told his disciples that after the Cross they would keep the Sabbath. Peter and Paul kept the Sabbath. The book of Revelation calls us back to worshipping the Creator each Sabbath.

Many Christians are confused over the expression 'the Lord's Day' in Revelation 1:10. John declares, 'On the Lord's Day I was in the Spirit.' What is the Lord's Day? Is there a difference between the Lord's Day and the Bible Sabbath? Are these two different days – one for the Old Testament and the other for the New Testament – or are they the same day?

We may attempt to give our twist to the meaning of the Lord's Day, but Jesus knows what he meant by his expression 'Lord's Day' better than we do. Let's allow Jesus to define the Lord's Day. 'For the Son of Man is *Lord of the Sabbath*.' (Matthew 12:8.) 'So the Son of Man is *Lord even of the Sabbath*.' (Mark 2:28.) 'The Son of Man is *Lord of the Sabbath*.' (Luke 6:5.)

Why do you think the Bible includes the same thing three times? There is only one reason. It is of vital importance.

And if 'The Son of Man is Lord of the Sabbath', then the Sabbath must be the Lord's Day. The Sabbath of the Creator God in Genesis is the Lord's Day of Revelation.

He's the same Creator in Revelation as he was in

Genesis. Just as he declared to the first inhabitants of the earth, 'I blessed, sanctified and rested upon the Sabbath,' he calls all humanity to worship him as Creator in the end time. He does not change. Revelation describes God's last day people in these words, 'This calls for patient endurance on the part of the saints who obey God's commandments and remain faithful to Jesus.' (Revelation 14:12.)

God's people awaiting his soon return will be keeping his commandments, including the seventh-day Sabbath. They will lovingly obey him. The Sabbath will be a symbol of true worship in the end time.

The Sabbath will be the symbol of true worship throughout all eternity. 'As the new heavens and the new earth that I make will endure before me, declares the LORD, so will your name and descendants endure. From one New Moon to another and from one Sabbath to another, all mankind will come and bow down before me, says the LORD.' (Isaiah 66:22, 23.)

From around the world they will come and together as one common humanity, together as brothers and sisters as one family, will give him praise, honour and glory.

Together we shall come to praise the Christ who created Heaven and Earth. We shall unite to praise the Father, Son and Holy Spirit. We shall come together to worship the Christ who died for us.

Maybe you are thinking, 'This is new to me.' But I know you have only one desire. You long to follow Jesus and do his will. When we learn God wrote the Ten Commandments with his own finger on tables of stone, and one of the commandments – only one – has the word *Remember*, we dare not forget what God said to remember. To forget to remember what God himself says is of utmost importance is to miss the enormous blessings of the Sabbath command. It is to miss experiencing the peace, rest and joy the Sabbath brings.

A day to remember

Throughout the Bible, the Sabbath command is plain.

The Sabbath is a sign between God and his people. All of the Old Testament believers kept the Sabbath. Peter, James and John kept the Sabbath. Paul taught a whole city to keep the Sabbath. All of the New Testament believers kept the Sabbath.

Jesus himself worshipped the Father every Sabbath. Jesus said, 'If you love me, you will obey what I command.' (John 14:15.) When we discover the marvellous beauty of the Sabbath, our hearts are broken with love for Christ. We cry from the depths of our being, 'I will follow you, my Saviour. Even if it's different from popular opinion; even if it's different from what conventional religion teaches, my heart wants only one thing – Bible truth. My heart wants only one thing, Jesus.'

Just now, would you like to bow your head and say, 'Jesus, teach me your truth. Wherever it leads me I will follow'?

Would you like to say, 'Dear Jesus, I want to follow you, no matter what others teach. I want to worship you as Creator and Lord and every week discover your Sabbath rest'?

For me, the most important thing in life is to follow Jesus. Is this your desire? Is this your commitment? Is Jesus' will more important to you than anything else in this life? Would you like me to pray Jesus will guide you into doing his will today and always?

Why don't you open your heart right now and say, 'Yes, Jesus, I will do your will.'

——— Chapter four ———

History's greatest hoax

Have you ever noticed that things aren't always what they appear to be? For centuries, scientists believed that the earth was the stationary centre of the universe, and everything, including the sun and stars, orbited around it. It was a free-thinking Polish man, Copernicus, who determined that the earth was itself in motion and revolved around the sun. He compared how sailors in a ship on a calm sea might experience the illusion of being perfectly still, with everything else around them moving.

'In the same way,' Copernicus wrote, 'the motion of the earth can unquestionably produce the impression that the entire universe is rotating.'

Simply because it *appeared* that the sun and stars were moving around the earth didn't mean they were. Merely because you believe something doesn't make it true.

Merely because something is believed for centuries doesn't make it true. Could it be that a tradition like one of those long-held ideas slipped into the Christian Church?

Is it possible that millions have accepted falsehood in the place of truth and very few question it? Do you think it's possible that most churches have set aside a commandment of God to follow human tradition instead? Could it be that this tradition has been around so long that it is accepted as truth when it is solely of human origin? This is all part of Satan's plan to deceive

History's greatest hoax

God's people in the last days.

Counterfeit

The book of Revelation predicts that Satan would attempt to mislead the Christian Church. Consider this amazing statement in Revelation: 'The great dragon was hurled down – that ancient serpent called the devil, or Satan, who leads the whole world astray.' (Revelation 12:9.) He's a serpent. He deceived Eve in the Garden of Eden. He's deceived men and women down through the ages.

His deceptions are so cunning, so powerful, that he attempts to thrust them upon the entire world. The Bible says, 'He was hurled to the earth, and his angels with him.' (Revelation 12:9, last part.)

Satan is a deceiver. Wouldn't it be logical for Satan to try to palm off a religious counterfeit? The value of a counterfeit is that it looks as much like the genuine as possible. No counterfeiter in the world would seriously make a counterfeit £3 or £13 note. Why not? Simply because there is no genuine. Satan's strategy is to counterfeit divine truth and especially attack God's commandments. Now isn't it logical that Satan the great deceiver would attack God's law?

God's law represents God's authority. If Satan can do away with God's law, he can do away with God's authority. God's law is the foundation of his government. God's law defines what's right and what's wrong. And if Satan could deceive God's people over the subject of the law, he could undermine the entire foundation of God's throne. He could undermine God's power, God's credibility and God's authority. But right in the heart of God's law is the Sabbath. Now isn't it logical that Satan the great deceiver would attack the Creator by challenging the symbol of Creation, the Sabbath? Have you begun to wonder how the Bible Sabbath was changed from the seventh day (Saturday) to the first day (Sunday)?

If the Bible is so clear on this topic, why are so many people confused? Who changed the Sabbath? When was it changed? And why was it changed? There are certainly good answers to these questions. The answers come from both the Bible and history.

One thing is for certain – God did not change the Sabbath. The prophet Malachi quotes God's words this way, 'I the LORD do not change' (Malachi 3:6).

There are honest-hearted, sincere people who read the Genesis account of Creation and discover God blessed the seventh day and sanctified it. They also find he rested on the seventh-day Sabbath. They read that God established the Sabbath in the days of Adam, more than two thousand years before the existence of the Jewish race.

These truth-seeking Christians read the Ten Commandments written with God's own finger and come across the fourth commandment, 'Remember the Sabbath day, to keep it holy. Six days you shall labour and do all your work, but the seventh day is the Sabbath of the LORD your God.' (Exodus 20:8-10, NKJV.)

They're confused; the church that they're attending keeps Sunday. They are perplexed because they read the Sabbath commandment and it is so clear. They read in Ezekiel 20:12, 'I gave them my sabbaths, as a sign between me and them . . .' (NRSV). They see that the Sabbath is a sign between God and his people. It has been God's sign down through the centuries. These sincere Christians read in Luke 4:16 that Jesus, as his custom was, went to church on the Sabbath.

They read that Christ affirmed in Matthew 24:20 that his disciples would be keeping the Sabbath forty years after the Cross. They read in Acts 13:42-44 that the apostle Paul taught a whole city to keep the Sabbath.

They read in Revelation 1:10 that the Lord has a day. And they read in Luke 6:5 that the Sabbath is the Lord's Day. They read the same thing in Mark 2:27, 28

History's greatest hoax

and Matthew 12:8.

Who changed the Sabbath?

These Christians ask, 'Who changed the Sabbath?' They see that God didn't change it, for he declares, 'I the LORD do not change' (Malachi 3:6). Then they look at the Bible and they discover Jesus didn't change the Sabbath, for 'Jesus Christ is the same yesterday, today and forever.' (Hebrews 13:8.)

The teachings of Jesus are timeless. The doctrines he taught are eternal. Jesus certainly would not tamper with his Father's law and he certainly did not give his disciples the authority to change it either.

Listen to Peter's comments to the Roman authorities, 'But Peter and the other apostles replied: We must obey God rather than men.' (Acts 5:29.) So the question then is, if God didn't change the Sabbath, if Jesus wouldn't change the Sabbath, if the disciples couldn't change the Sabbath, who did it?

In the book of Revelation, chapter 13, we read about a 'beast' that rises up out of the sea. This beast is also known as the antichrist.

The entire world follows the 'beast's' deceptions. In Revelation 13 there is fascinating imagery. 'And I saw a beast coming out of the sea. He had ten horns and seven heads, with ten crowns on his horns, and on each head a blasphemous name.' (Revelation 13:1.)

A 'beast' in the Bible is a king or a kingdom (Daniel 7:17, 23). It can be a political or a religious power or kingdom. This 'beast' rose up out of the sea. The sea represents peoples or nations (Revelation 17:15).

This power that arises is a blasphemous power. In the Bible, blasphemy occurs when an earthly power or human being assumes the privileges and prerogatives of God. (See John 10:33.)

One aspect of blasphemy is claiming to have the authority to change the very law written with God's own finger. Here's why. If an earthly power has the authority

to change God's law, it must be greater than the one who gave the law in the first place. If God's law is the eternal foundation of his government, an attempt to change the law is an attack on the lawgiver. Any attempt to change God's law exalts the one making the change above God, and that is blasphemy. And then there is this imagery in Revelation 13:2: 'The beast I saw resembled a leopard, but had feet like those of a bear and a mouth like that of a lion. The dragon gave the beast his power and his throne and great authority.'

To understand what's coming in the future it becomes imperative to understand these symbols of the lion, the bear, the leopard and the dragon. It also becomes necessary to understand that the battle in the universe between good and evil is a battle over worship. It centres on God's law. The Sabbath is at the heart of this controversy over worship.

Unity of Church and state

To understand Revelation, it is first necessary to understand Daniel. The prophecies of Daniel are linked to the prophecies of Revelation. Let's go back to Daniel, the seventh chapter. We have the same imagery as Revelation 13; the lion, the bear, the leopard and the dragon. Here in Daniel 7 we have a description of a power that would rise in the early centuries. It would unite Church and state.

This religious power would usurp God's authority. It claimed that it had the power to change God's law. Let's discover *who* this power is, *where* this power arose and *what* this power did.

Let's survey the prophecies in the Bible that predict this power would attempt to change God's law.

Let's open up the pages of history and read its own claims that it has sufficient authority to change God's Sabbath.

As you continue to read, you will understand, possibly for the first time in your life, the central issues in this conflict over worship and why the Sabbath is so important to God. You will also understand how Sunday came into the Christian Church.

It's an absolutely amazing journey as we compare Bible prophecy with the annals of history.

One night as the prophet Daniel fell asleep he had a dream. The Bible describes his dream in Daniel 7:2, 3. 'Daniel said: In my vision at night I looked, and there before me were the four winds of heaven churning up the great sea. Four great beasts, each different from the others, came up out of the sea.'

Four kingdoms

Four beasts arise from the sea. They are different from each other. What does a 'beast' represent in Bible prophecy?

'The four great beasts are four kingdoms that will rise from the earth.' (Daniel 7:17.)

'The fourth beast is a fourth kingdom that will appear on earth.' (Daniel 7:23.) These four beasts represent four kingdoms. These four world-ruling kingdoms which begin in Daniel's day take us down the stream of time.

In Daniel chapter 7 these four great world-ruling empires are pictured or described as wild beasts. In Daniel chapter 2 these same world-ruling empires are portrayed as metals of varied worth and strength.

Babylon

In Daniel chapter 2, King Nebuchadnezzar of Babylon dreamed of a great image.

The image had a head of gold, chest and arms of silver, thighs of bronze, legs of iron, and feet of iron and clay. We do not have to guess at the meaning of this giant statue composed of four metals. Speaking of the golden head, Daniel declares, 'You [Nebuchadnezzar] are that head of gold. After you, another kingdom will rise, inferior to yours. Next, a third kingdom, one of

bronze, will rule over the whole earth. Finally, there will be a fourth kingdom, strong as iron . . .' (Daniel 2:38-40).

Babylon, the first of these four kingdoms, was named directly by Daniel. He also names the empire which overthrew Babylon – Medo-Persia (Daniel 5:28-30), and the nation which over threw Medo-Persia – Greece (Daniel 8:20, 21).

The four metals in the image represented four world-ruling powers – Babylon, Medo-Persia, Greece and Rome.

The image had feet of iron mixed with clay, which represented divided Europe, and a rock cut out without human hands smashed the image. This rock represents Jesus, the Rock of Ages, who will one day destroy the kingdoms of this world and establish his eternal, everlasting Kingdom.

Let's look at it carefully and see how these animal figures of Daniel 7 represent these ancient nations.

And then let's come to the days of Christ and early Christianity and see how a power emerged that attempted to change God's Sabbath.

Let's look at how the Bible predicts what would happen and see clearly how history confirms what actually happened. As these prophetic beasts stride across the landscape of time, we see the unfolding of history. 'The first was like a lion, and it had the wings of an eagle. I watched until its wings were torn off and it was lifted from the ground so that it stood on two feet like a man, and the heart of a man was given to it.' (Daniel 7:4.)

The first beast was like a lion with eagle's wings. Where is Babylon? Babylon is in the modern country of Iraq. It's about 60 miles south of Baghdad. When the archaeologists were digging in Iraq, they found engravings on Babylon's walls of a lion with eagle's wings.

The lion with eagle's wings was a well-known

History's greatest hoax

symbol of Babylon. In Daniel's day Babylon was a mighty world-dominating power.

Then another nation was to rise. Babylon wouldn't 'rule the world' forever. 'And there before me was a second beast, which looked like a bear. It was raised up on one of its sides, and it had three ribs in its mouth between its teeth.' (Daniel 7:5.)

Medo-Persia
Now notice that the second empire is like a bear that raises itself up on one side. Medo-Persia overthrew Babylon.

The bear of Medo-Persia, raising itself up on one side, represented the Persians overthrowing first Babylon and then dominating the Medes. What does the bear have in its mouth? Three ribs. When Medo-Persia conquered the world, it first conquered Babylon, and then it went northward and conquered Lydia, then southward and conquered Egypt. These three nations, Babylon, Lydia and Egypt, represent the three ribs. Bible prophecy is extremely accurate. It is absolutely fantastic. A third empire rises: 'After that, I looked, and there before me was another beast, one that looked like a leopard. And on its back it had four wings like those of a bird. This beast had four heads, and it was given authority to rule.' (Daniel 7:6.)

Greece
The Greeks overthrew the Medes and the Persians.

What do you know about Greece? Who was the Greek leader? Alexander the Great. How old was he when he conquered, the world? He was in his early thirties, wasn't he?

Greece conquered the world quickly. If you wanted to describe rapid conquest, what animal would you choose that can really move fast? A leopard. But if you wanted to describe rapid, rapid, rapid conquest, what would you do with your leopard? You would put wings

on him.

God put wings on his leopard to describe the rapid conquest of Alexander the Great.

Why the four heads? Notice once again how accurate Bible prophecy is. Alexander the Great died very young at only 33 years old.

The four heads of the leopard represent Alexander's four generals who divided up the empire. Their names were Cassander, Lysimachus, Ptolemy and Seleucus.

Alexander the Great's four generals ruled exactly as Bible prophecy predicted.

Rome

The Bible describes a fourth empire: 'After that, in my vision at night I looked, and there before me was a fourth beast – terrifying and frightening and very powerful. It had large iron teeth; it crushed and devoured its victims and trampled underfoot whatever was left. It was different from all the former beasts, and it had ten horns.' (Daniel 7:7.)

It is very clear that this fourth beast represents the Roman Empire. This period takes us to the time of Christ. It was a Roman decree that brought Joseph to the town of Jesus' birth in Bethlehem.

It was Pontius Pilate, a Roman, who tried Jesus. It was a Roman soldier who nailed Jesus to the Cross.

Rome ruled the world in the days of Jesus. Christianity grew up in this Roman Empire. The Bible describes the collapse of the Roman Empire clearly in the symbolism of the toes of the image and the horns of the fourth beast.

Divided Europe

The image of Daniel 2 had feet and toes of iron and clay, representing divided Europe.

The fourth beast here has ten horns. Rome was divided into ten main divisions. The barbarian tribes swept across the empire, pillaging and plundering,

History's greatest hoax

destroying villages and occupying cities. The Roman Empire was divided. These divisions are revealed in the ten horns of this beast. Then God reveals how apostasy would enter the Church at a time when the Roman Empire was being overrun by the barbarian tribes from the north.

'The little horn'?

This prophecy in Daniel chapter 7 clearly reveals the conflict over worship and precisely how the Sabbath was changed.

As Daniel, in vision, viewed these ten horns he saw something else remarkable arise. 'While I was thinking about the horns, there before me was another horn, a little one, which came up among them; and three of the first horns were uprooted before it. This horn had eyes like the eyes of a man and a mouth that spoke boastfully.' (Daniel 7:8.)

The Bible says this little horn arose and was different from all the rest. Who is this little horn rising up among the ten horns? Let's try to find out some things the Bible says about this mysterious little horn.

* First, this little horn comes up among the first ten (Daniel 7:8). If the ten horns are divisions of Rome, this little horn has to come up in Western Europe.

This little horn doesn't come up in Asia, Africa or North or South America. Its roots are in European soil.

* Secondly, the Bible says, this little horn would rise up *after* the ten horns (Daniel 7:8).

It doesn't come up in the days of Babylon, Medo-Persia, Greece or Rome. It comes up after the fall of the Roman Empire. It comes up when Rome is being divided. It's a power that rises out of Rome in the early centuries.

As we shall see, this power would think to change the very law of God.

* The Bible also says thirdly that this little horn has eyes like the eyes of a man. What does this represent?

Do you know what a prophet is called in the Bible? In the Bible, a prophet is called a 'seer' because a prophet sees with God's eyes.

The eyes of a man represent not divine wisdom but human wisdom. It is a human religious system based on man's teachings which would rise out of Rome.

Notice the Bible says in Daniel 7:24 that it is different from all the rest. This is the fourth clue to understanding this little horn. 'After them another king will arise, different from the earlier ones' (Daniel 7:24).

All the other powers before it, Babylon, Medo-Persia, Greece and Rome, were political powers. This one is different. It is not primarily a political power; *it is a religious power – a religio-political power.*

What would this power do? It would attempt to change the very law of God.

A counterfeit Sabbath

Notice what the Bible says in Daniel 7:25: 'He will speak against the Most High and oppress his saints and try to change the set times and the laws.'

Can you think of any greater way of speaking 'against the Most High' than an attempt to change God's law, especially his Sabbath?

This power would attempt to change the very law of God. This is obviously speaking about divine laws. It's not speaking about something insignificant like tax laws or political laws. When one nation follows another, it nearly always changes human laws. There's nothing surprising about that or anything different from the other beasts. But this little horn power would speak great words against the Most High by assuming God's prerogative and attempting to change divine laws.

Now notice the Bible doesn't say it *could* change those laws; it would only *try* to change them. It would make it appear that it had changed them.

No earthly power, however mighty it claims to be, could ever change God's law. This power would think it had the authority to change God's law.

This power would attempt to change the very law of God. How could this possibly take place? Daniel 8:12 tells us that this little horn power 'cast truth to the ground, and kept prospering in what it did.' (NRSV.)

Daniel's prophecy predicts that a powerful religious power would rise out of the old Roman Empire. This power would be small at first but would become extremely powerful.

It would claim that it had the authority to change the very law of God. How did the change from Sabbath to Sunday actually occur? What happened historically?

Let's briefly review what we have studied so far in Daniel 7. The four beasts represented the four world-ruling empires of Babylon, Medo-Persia, Greece and Rome. The little horn which arises out of the Roman Empire arises with a man as its leader in the early centuries of the Christian Church. In an attempt to appease the pagans entering the Church in large numbers and make Christianity more acceptable in the empire, this Roman power would attempt to change God's law. The change of the Sabbath occurred gradually over a period of time. It resulted in a variety of social and religious factors.

Dr John Eadie helps us to understand the roots of this change in his *Bible Encyclopaedia*. He says: 'Sabbath . . . A Hebrew word signifying rest . . . Sunday was a name given by the heathens to the first day of the week, because it was the day on which they worshipped the sun.' (Page 561.)

Sun worship was common in Egypt, Babylon, Persia and Rome.

In the fourth century, the Roman emperor Constantine was also influenced by sun worship. Constantine desired to unite his empire.

How could the emperor unite his empire? Constantine passed a decree to provide a common day of rest and recreation throughout the empire. His clear intent was to

promote unity among the pagans and Christians throughout his realm.

'The venerable day of the sun'

Here is the emperor's decree from AD321. It commands, 'On the venerable day of the Sun let the magistrates and people residing in cities rest, and let all the shops be closed.'

Constantine calls Sunday 'the venerable day of the Sun'. He declares 'all workshops be closed'.

In an attempt to unite the empire, Constantine issued the first Sunday law. He was so inclined towards the sun god, he put his own image on one side of his coins and the sun god on the other!

In the days of Constantine Church and state united in an attempt to 'Christianise' the pagans and unite the empire. The Roman government and the Roman Church united. Here's an amazing statement, published in March of 1994 in the *Catholic World*. 'The sun was a foremost god with heathendom . . . there is, in truth, something royal, kingly about the sun, making it a fit emblem of Jesus, the Sun of Justice. Hence the Church in these countries would seem to have said, "Keep that old pagan name. It shall remain consecrated, sanctified." And thus the pagan Sunday, dedicated to Balder, became the Christian Sunday, sacred to Jesus.' (Page 809.)

Do you see how it happened? Do you see how Sunday came into the Church?

Constantine wanted to unite his empire, and Roman church leaders wanted to convert the pagans.

Sunday became the vehicle to accomplish both; so the biblical Sabbath was changed by the Roman Church and state. There was another issue at play here. The Roman Church wanted to distance itself from Judaism. There was an anti-Jewish sentiment in the Roman Empire. God didn't change the Sabbath. Jesus didn't change it. The disciples didn't change it.

History's greatest hoax

The Roman Church Council of Laodicea records the first prohibition of keeping the Bible Sabbath.

The bishops met at Laodicea and decreed, 'Christians shall not Judaize [that is, they shall not keep the Sabbath] and be idle on Saturday.' (Council of Laodicea, AD325.)

Here the church council is saying: We're forbidding Christians to rest on Sabbath. They shall work on that day. 'But the Lord's Day they shall especially honour, and as being Christians, shall, if possible, do no work on that day. If however they are found Judaizing [keeping the Sabbath] they shall be shut out from Christ.'

This statement is extremely significant for another reason. Christian leaders felt the Sabbath was 'Jewish' and wanted to disassociate themselves from the Jews due to an anti-Jewish feeling throughout the Roman Empire.

Here is a church council that unites with the Roman government under Constantine and attempts to shift the authority of Sabbath to Sunday.

The change of the Sabbath took place gradually as Christians distanced themselves from the Jews and church and state leaders joined hands to unite the empire. The Bible makes this plain. Daniel 7:25: 'He will . . . try to change the set times and the laws.'

Daniel 7:25 says that an earthly power growing up out of Rome would attempt to change God's law. God says beware! There are numerous statements from Roman sources which acknowledge that the Church changed the Sabbath. The *Convert's Catechism of Catholic Doctrine* asks:

Q. What is the third commandment?
A. The third commandment is: Remember that thou keep holy the Sabbath day.
Q. Which is the Sabbath day?
A. Saturday is the Sabbath day.
Q. Why do we observe Sunday instead of Saturday?

A. We observe Sunday instead of Saturday because the Catholic Church transferred the solemnity from Saturday to Sunday. (Peter Geiermann, *Convert's Catechism of Catholic Doctrine*, page 50.)

You may wonder why these statements from the Catholic catechism refer to the Sabbath commandment as the third commandment rather than the fourth. This is simply because the Roman Church dropped the second commandment on graven images and divided the tenth commandment, 'You shall not covet,' into two commands: 'You shall not covet your neighbour's wife and you shall not covet your neighbour's goods' so that there were still ten.

The law of God was 'changed' by the Roman Church in the fourth and fifth centuries. This is no secret. The Church openly admits it.

The *Catholic Mirror* of 23 September 1893 states, 'The Catholic church for over one thousand years before the existence of a Protestant, by virtue of her divine mission, changed the day from Saturday to Sunday.'

The *Catholic Encyclopaedia*, volume 4, page 153, adds, 'The church after changing the day of rest from the Jewish Sabbath of the seventh day of the week to the first made the third commandment refer to Sunday as the day to be kept holy as the Lord's Day.'

Here the Church openly acknowledges changing the Sabbath. The Sabbath, of course, was never an exclusively Jewish institution. It was always 'the Sabbath of the Lord'.

St Catherine's Catholic Church in Algonquin, Michigan, published a remarkable statement in its 21 May 1995 newsletter. 'Perhaps, the boldest thing, the most revolutionary thing the church ever did happened in the first century. The Holy day the Sabbath was changed from Saturday to Sunday. . . . Not from any command noted in scripture but from the church's sense of its own power.'

History's greatest hoax

Karl Keating, one of the foremost Catholic lay scholars in the United States today, wrote a book as a challenge to Protestants. He explained the change of the Sabbath this way. 'Fundamentalists meet for worship on Sunday, yet there is no evidence in the Bible that corporate worship was to be made on Sundays. The Jewish Sabbath, or day of rest was, of course, Saturday. It was the Catholic Church that decided Sunday should be the day of worship for Christians, in honour of the resurrection.' (*Catholicism and Fundamentalism*, page 38.)

This Catholic author is reasoning with Protestants. He says, if you want to follow the Bible you should keep the Bible Sabbath. He then argues that the Bible alone is not a sufficient guide without church authority and interpretation. The pastor of St Catherine's in Michigan reasoned the same way and then made this remarkable statement, 'People who think that the scriptures should be the sole authority should logically become Seventh-day Adventists and keep Saturday holy.' (*St Catherine Catholic Church Sentinel*, 21 May 1995.)

The central issue regarding the change of the Sabbath is: *Does the Church have the authority to change God's law?*

If you accept Sunday, you are accepting a day based on the authority of the Church. The argument of the Catholic Church is this: to accept Sunday is to accept the authority of the Church. If you accept the authority of the Catholic Church in changing the Sabbath, in all honesty you should be a Catholic.

Here is a quote from Cardinal James Gibbons, the foremost Catholic scholar in America in the nineteenth century. Writing in the latter part of that century, the cardinal declared, 'You may read the Bible from Genesis to Revelation, and you will not find a single line authorizing the sanctification of Sunday. The scriptures enforce the religious observance of Saturday,' *Faith of*

our Fathers, page 56.

The issues are much more than a matter of days. The issue is: What is our guide? Is it the Bible or is it tradition? The issue is: Does any human church or human religious leader, for whatever reason or motive, have the authority to change God's law that was written with his finger on those tables of stone?

Has God given any church, any human being, the authority to change his law? Has he done that?

Not at all! And so the issue is one of authority. God says, 'I will not violate my covenant, or alter the word that went forth from my lips.' (Psalm 89:34, NRSV.)

In the *Toronto Daily Star*, 26 October 1949, a Protestant Anglican bishop shocked the entire Protestant world.

The *Toronto Daily Star* reported the following story. 'Reverend Philip Carrington, Anglican Archbishop of Quebec, sent local clergymen into a huddle today by saying outright that there was nothing to support Sunday being kept holy. Carrington definitely told a church meeting in this city of straight-laced Protestantism that tradition, not the Bible, made Sunday the day of worship.'

You see what the issue is? It's not a matter of days. It's a matter of authority. Is it Jesus or the leaders of the church? What is the foundation of your faith? Is it the Bible or is it tradition? In the 1500s, in the days of the Reformation, Martin Luther argued before the priests and prelates of Europe that the Bible and the Bible only was the Christian's rule of faith and practice. He affirmed, 'My conscience is bound by the word of God.' Dr Johann Maier von Eck was the brilliant Catholic scholar enlisted by the church to debate with Luther.

One of the arguments Dr Eck used against Martin Luther revolved around the Sabbath. He suggested that the authority of the Church could therefore not be bound to the authority of the Scriptures because the church had changed 'the Sabbath to Sunday, not by

History's greatest hoax

the command of Christ but by its own authority.'
(Holtzman, *Canon and Tradition*, page 263.) The issue
surrounding the Sabbath is one of authority. Dr Eck's
argument against Luther's famous declaration of 'the
Bible and the Bible only', *sola scriptura*, was simple.
Tradition supersedes the Bible, and the fact Luther
accepted Sunday was proof enough for Eck that Luther
did not fully accept all of the Bible, but in Sunday
accepted the authority of the Roman Catholic Church.

When you really love Christ he is your final authority.
His Word is your guide. Some things are matters of
personal opinion; a change in God's law is not.

To give up the Bible Sabbath, given by God as a
sign of his creative authority, does matter, friend. A
change in God's law matters a great deal.

* I would much rather follow what God gave to
Adam and Eve in the Garden of Eden. What about
you?

* I would much rather follow what God gave to
Moses in the Ten Commandments.

* I'd much rather follow the example of Jesus Christ
himself.

God says the Sabbath is his great sign. It's a sign of
our loyalty to Christ. It is a sign we believe he created
our world.

It's the sign that we want to follow all his Word. In the
last days of earth history, God's Word says: 'Here is a
call for the endurance of the saints, those who keep the
commandments of God and hold fast to the faith of
Jesus.' (Revelation 14:12, NRSV.)

In the last days God will have a group of people who
love Jesus. They love him so much that they obey him.
It's more than a matter of days. In the Garden of Eden
Satan said to Eve, 'What difference does a tree make?
All trees are alike.' And Eve lost Eden because she
bought into that lie.

And many Christians today are buying into a
deception. People say, 'What difference does a day

make? All days are alike.' With God all days are not alike. One day was blessed by God, the seventh. One day was sanctified by God, set aside – the seventh day. And God rested on only one day – the Sabbath.

The issues that we are dealing with are issues of authority. Issues of obedience. Our choice is:

- The Bible or tradition
- Jesus or religious leaders
- God's law or man's dogmas
- God's instruction or human teaching
- God's way or man's way

And God says to you and to me right now, 'Choose for yourselves this day whom you will serve, . . . But as for me and my household, we will serve the LORD.' (Joshua 24:15.)

Will you say, 'Yes, I choose Jesus. I choose his way. I choose lovingly to obey his law'?

Now the question is sometimes asked, 'Are you suggesting that everybody who keeps Sunday is lost?'

Let me make it plain. Everybody who keeps Sunday is *not* lost. There are many Sunday-keeping Christians who love Jesus Christ. They are living up to all the light they know. When they learn more they are willing to follow it.

All over the world tens of thousands are hearing God's call and stepping out for his truth.

Would you like to respond by saying, 'Yes, Lord, you have revealed your truth and, like Joshua, I choose to follow you. I want to follow Jesus today.'

Jesus is calling you to step out of the crowd.

Why not bow your head and make your commitment to follow him right now?

An advance on eternity

The casualties on both sides were high. The shelling was intense. Heavy bombardment from the artillery lasted all day. The ground shook violently from the incessant pounding of the enemy aircraft. The Allied Forces responded with a fire fight of their own. Rival armies faced each other across the trenches.

Joe, an 18-year-old 'tommy', leaned back against the earthen wall of his freshly-dug trench, exhausted. The sun was setting. Another day passed and he was still alive. It was Christmas Eve. Thoughts of home flooded into his mind. . . .

Mum, Dad . . . his sister Alice . . . freshly baked apple pie . . . colourfully wrapped presents . . . the Christmas tree . . . smiles . . . hugs . . . logs burning in the fireplace . . . peace. But in this nightmare called war, death stared him in the face. 'Peace on earth and good will toward men' were only figments of his imagination.

The battlefield was quiet now. The air was crisp and clear. The stars twinkled in a moonlit sky. Then he heard it. Could it really be singing? Were his ears deceiving him this Christmas Eve? Was this some kind of subtle trap?

The sounds of a familiar Christmas carol gladdened the night air. Although the words were German, the tune was unmistakable. 'Silent night, holy night.' German soldiers sang Christmas carols a few hundred yards away in full view. Slowly, cautiously at first, Joe

pulled himself out of his foxhole. His heart was touched. His emotions were stirred. Suddenly he couldn't restrain himself any longer. Spontaneously he, too, began singing.

'Silent night, holy night, All is calm, All is bright.' His fellow Brits joined in the singing. Soon voices which a few hours before had shouted the curses of war now echoed a chorus of praise. The two opposing sides approached each other. They embraced. They laughed. They sang. For one night they were brothers. They shared a common humanity. The fighting stopped. The bombing ceased. The mortars were silent. On that Christmas Eve for just a brief moment, enemies became friends. In a sense, they recognised a profound truth expressed in Acts 17:24, 26.

'The God who made the world and everything in it is the Lord of heaven and earth and does not live in temples built by hands. . . . From one man he made every nation of men, that they should inhabit the whole earth; and he determined the times set for them and the exact places where they should live.'

The essence of humanity's dignity is a common creation. The fact that we are uniquely created by God places value on every human being. God is our Father. Ours is a shared heritage. We are sons and daughters of the King. We belong to the same family. We are brothers and sisters fashioned, shaped and moulded by the same God.

Creation provides a true sense of self-worth. The Creator of the universe made us. Each one of us is special in his sight. When the genes and chromosomes came together to form the unique structure of your personality, God threw away the pattern. There is no one else like you in all the universe. You are unique – a one-of-a-kind creation.

Evolution is dehumanising. If I am an enlarged protein molecule, if I am simply the product of fortuitous chance, if I am only an advanced form of the

An advance on eternity

animal creation, life has little meaning. I am merely one of six billion people clawing at one another for living space on a planet called Earth. Creation provides a moral imperative for living. I have been created by God and I am accountable to him for my actions. The One who made me holds me responsible. He has established 'absolutes in the world of moral relativism'.

Evolution provides no moral ethic for living. Since humans are advanced animals, the highest standard is the human mind. Morality is determined from within. There is no absolute, eternal standard to govern behaviour.

Creation provides a sense of hope. The God who created me loves me. He cares for me. He will guide me throughout this life.

Evolution looks within to find strength for life's trials. Creation looks without. It looks to a loving, powerful, all-knowing God. Creation provides a sense of destiny. The God who loves me, who created me, who cares for me has prepared a place in Heaven for me. Death is not a long night without a morning. The grave is not some dark hole in the ground. God has a glorious new tomorrow planned.

For the evolutionist death is the end. There is no tomorrow. Creation speaks of hope. Evolution echoes death. Creation speaks of a certain future. Evolution echoes blind chance. Creation answers the eternal questions of life. Where did I come from? Why am I here? Where am I going? Evolution provides a distorted view of life's origin, fails to address the question of life's purpose, and leaves the soul barren regarding life's ultimate destiny. Creation unites us with God. It establishes our self-worth. It forges ties with all humanity. It creates a common ancestry. It inspires confidence in a God who cares. It links us to God's inexhaustible power and it encourages us with the hope of life after death.

When God said REMEMBER

Creation and the Sabbath

It is because our world so desperately needs the reassuring message of Creation that God gave us the Sabbath.

In the mid-1800s when the evolutionary hypothesis was taking the intellectual world by storm, God sent a message of incredible hope. It is found in Revelation 14:6, 7.

'Then I saw another angel flying in mid-air, and he had the eternal gospel to proclaim to those who live on the earth – to every nation, tribe, language and people. He said in a loud voice, Fear God and give him glory, because the hour of his judgement has come. Worship him who made the heavens, the earth, the sea and the springs of water.'

What do we call the One who made Heaven, Earth and sea? The Creator. Heaven's final appeal to mankind in the Bible's last book, Revelation, calls us to worship the Creator.

God's last-day message is one that calls all humanity back to worshipping him as the One who made Heaven and Earth. The basis of all worship is the fact that God created us. Accept evolution and you destroy the very basis for worship. John the Revelator succinctly states it in these words, 'You are worthy, our Lord and God, to receive glory and honour and power, for you created all things, and by your will they were created and have their being.' (Revelation 4:11.)

He is worthy precisely because he has created. If God did not create us, if we merely evolved and life is a cosmic accident based on chance and random selection, there is absolutely no reason to worship.

In an age of evolution, God has given the Sabbath as an eternal symbol of his creative power and authority. The Sabbath is a weekly reminder that we are not our own. He created us. Life cannot exist apart from him.

'In him we live and move and have our being.' (Acts 17:28.)

An advance on eternity

The Sabbath calls us back to our roots. It's a link to our family of origin. The Sabbath has been observed continuously since time began. It is an unbroken connection back through time to our Creator. The Sabbath tells us that we are not just a product of matter plus time plus chance. It keeps us focused on the glorious truth that we are children of God. It calls us to an intimate, close relationship with him.

When Schia was 4 years old, her baby brother was born. Little Schia began to ask her parents to leave her alone with the new baby. They worried that like some 4 year olds she might be jealous and shake or hit the baby, so they said no! Over time, though, since Schia wasn't showing signs of jealousy, they changed their minds and decided to let Schia have her private conference with 'Baby'. Elated, Schia went into the baby's room and shut the door, but it opened a crack, enough for her curious parents to peek in and listen. They saw little Schia walk quietly up to her baby brother, put her face close to his and say, 'Baby, tell me what God feels like. I am starting to forget.'

The truth is, we all tend to forget. That's why God says, 'Remember.' The Sabbath is a weekly reminder of what God is like. It calls us to a new relationship with him.

A not-so-subtle deception

In an attempt to destroy the uniqueness of our creation, the devil has introduced a not-so-subtle counterfeit. This counterfeit, which is accepted by some well-meaning Christians, attempts to harmonise Creation and evolution. Their reasoning goes something like this: God is the prime cause of Creation, but he took long ages to bring the world into existence. This approach attempts to harmonise so-called 'scientific data' with the Genesis account. It asserts that the days of creation are long, indefinite periods of time. It accepts the evolutionary viewpoint and creates far

more problems than it solves. It completely disregards the psalmist's statement, 'By the word of the LORD were the heavens made, their starry host by the breath of his mouth. . . . For he spoke, and it came to be; he commanded, and it stood firm.' (Psalm 33:6, 9.)

It overlooks the clear declaration of Hebrews 11:3, 'By faith we understand that the universe was formed at God's command, so that what is seen was not made out of what was visible.'

The Bible teaches that God created the world in six literal days of twenty-four hours and rested the seventh. The linguistic structure of Genesis 1 and 2 does not permit anything else. The Hebrew word for day is *Yom*. Throughout the Bible, every time a number precedes the word *Yom* as an adjective, it limits the time period to twenty-four hours. There is not a single instance in the Bible when a numeral precedes the noun *Yom*, and *Yom* indicates an indefinite period. Without exception, it is always a twenty-four-hour period. To accept the false idea of long, indefinite periods of creation is to challenge the precise language of Scripture. It is to superimpose our personal opinion upon the grammatical structure of God's Word. If the writer of Genesis desired to communicate that the world took millions of years to evolve, he would certainly have used different language.

Furthermore, if God did not create the world in six literal days, what significance does the seventh-day Sabbath have? How could God command, 'Remember the Sabbath day by keeping it holy. . . . For in six days the LORD made the heavens and the earth, the sea, and all that is in them, but he rested on the seventh day. Therefore the LORD blessed the Sabbath day and made it holy'? (Exodus 20:8-10.)

It would make absolutely no sense at all to leave the seventh day Sabbath as an eternal memorial of a six-day creation week if a six-day creation week never happened. To accept long ages of creation is to

An advance on eternity

challenge the very need for the seventh-day Sabbath. It is to challenge the authority of the Bible. It is to raise serious questions regarding the integrity of Scripture.

Satan is challenging the very heart of God's authority by attacking the Sabbath. The Sabbath is not merely good advice. It is a command from the very throne of God. To disregard the Sabbath, to treat the Sabbath as common, ordinary or as any other day is to miss a vital aspect of our faith relationship with God.

The Sabbath has been given to us by a loving Creator to unite us with him. The heart of the Sabbath is relationship – the acknowledgement that God is worthy of our supremest devotion, our deepest allegiance and our total loyalty.

The Sabbath and salvation

There is another sense in which the Sabbath speaks courage to our weary hearts. It shows us that we can rest in Christ for our salvation. The Sabbath is a symbol of his rest, not our works. It is a meaningful symbol of righteousness by faith, not legalism. It is a clarion call to trust in him, not in ourselves.

The writer of Hebrews uses the Sabbath as an illustration of this rest in Christ. He declares, 'There remains, then, a Sabbath-rest for the people of God; for anyone who enters God's rest also rests from his own work, just as God did from his.' (Hebrews 4:9, 10.)

Entering into true Sabbath rest means that we cease trying to create salvation on the basis of our own efforts. God has saved us in Christ. When Jesus voluntarily poured out his life on the Cross, he died the death we deserve. He gave his perfect life as a substitute for our sinful life. The Sabbath is not a symbol of legalism. It is rather an eternal reminder that we rest in him for our salvation.

The Carpenter from Nazareth built a special dwelling for us. We can find refuge there. We can be safe there. His work is complete. It is finished. We can know that in

Christ we are accepted by our loving heavenly Father. When we rest on the Sabbath, we are resting in his grace. We are resting in his righteousness. We are resting in his salvation.

Sabbath rest is a symbol of a faith experience in Jesus. It is a graphic illustration of our trust in him. All week we work, but on the seventh day we rest. We turn from our works to a total rest in Christ. In Jesus, we have somewhere to belong. We need not stressfully work out our own salvation. Our lives need not be filled with guilt and fear and anxiety. The Sabbath reveals a restful attitude. Salvation comes only through Jesus. We do not deserve it. We cannot earn it. We rest and receive it by faith.

When Jesus breathed his last and cried, 'It is finished,' he closed his eyes and died. The work of redemption was complete. He rested on the Sabbath, symbolising a completed or finished work.

At the end of creation week, God rested. His work of creating this world was finished. Each Sabbath, as we rest on the last day of the week, we, too, declare, 'God, I am resting in the completed work of Christ on the Cross. "Nothing in my hand I bring. Simply to thy cross I cling." '

There is still more that rounds out the picture. The prophet Ezekiel declares, 'Also I gave them my Sabbaths as a sign between us, so they would know that I the LORD made them holy.' (Ezekiel 20:12.)

Here's another reason why God gave us the Sabbath. It shows that the Lord is the One who sanctifies us. How is that? Well, that's what God did to the seventh day. It was an ordinary slice of time, just like any other at the end of creation week, but God set this particular day apart. He sanctified it. And through the Sabbath God tells us, 'That's what I want to do for you, too. I want to set you apart as my special child. I want to pour myself into you. I want to sanctify you. I want to share my holiness with you.'

An advance on eternity

The Sabbath reminds us of where we develop character – in relationship with our heavenly Father and with Jesus Christ. The Sabbath is a continual, living promise of God's ability to help us grow through all the ups and downs, tragedies and triumphs of our lives. We need that distinctive time with the heavenly Father. We need Sabbath quality time with the God who sanctifies us, the God who helps us keep growing.

The Sabbath has continued in the weekly cycle from the dawn of Creation until now. The Sabbath began in the Garden of Eden, and the Sabbath will be celebrated when this earth is renewed after Christ's Second Coming. The prophet Isaiah talks about the time when God will make the 'new heavens and the new earth'. He says: 'From one New Moon to another and from one Sabbath to another, all mankind will come and bow down before me, says the LORD.' (Isaiah 66:23.)

The Sabbath beautifully represents a forever relationship with God. It stretches from the Garden of Eden at Creation to the garden that God will make of this planet at the end of time. It stretches from Paradise lost to Paradise restored. We need that kind of forever in our lives. We need a place that reassures us that we are in an eternal relationship with the heavenly Father. We need a palace in time where that assurance can sink in deep, a place that says our heavenly Father will always be there for us. In the Sabbath, we can find a sense of contented rest. We can get in touch with our roots as his children there. We can grow and mature there. Yes, we need that kind of forever place that ties the whole of our lives to an eternal relationship with God.

Reader's Digest wrote of the late Harvey Penick, 'For ninety-year-old golf pro, Harvey Penick, success has come late.' His first golf book, *Harvey Penick's Little Red Book*, sold more than a million copies. His publisher, Simon and Schuster, believes the book is

one of the biggest selling sports books of all time. The story of the book's publishing is fascinating. Harvey Penick certainly didn't write it for the money.

In the 1920s Penick bought a red spiral notebook and began jotting down his personal observations regarding golf. He never showed the book to anyone except his son for nearly seventy years. In 1991 he shared it with a local writer and asked the man if he thought it was worth publishing. The writer was elated. He contacted the publishing giant Simon and Schuster immediately. The next evening the publishers agreed to a £50,000 advance. The jubilant writer passed the news on to Penick's wife.

When the writer saw Penick later in the evening, the old man seemed troubled. Something was seriously bothering him. Finally he came clean. With all of his medical bills, there was no way he could advance Simon and Schuster that much money to publish the book. The writer had to explain that Penick would be the one to receive the money.

An advance of £50,000 was his and he didn't even realise it. In the Sabbath, God has given us an 'advance' on eternity. Every Sabbath Heaven touches Earth. As the Jewish author Abraham Herschel so aptly put it, 'The Sabbath is a palace in time.' The Sabbath calls us from the things of time to the things of eternity.

It calls us to enter into his heavenly rest. It calls us to experience a foretaste of Heaven today. It calls us to a relationship with our Creator that will continue throughout eternity. The Sabbath is in actuality an advance on eternity. There is much more coming, but in the Sabbath we have the first instalment.

Is it possible that in their 'busyness' millions of people are missing one of life's greatest blessings?

Could it be that in our frantic quest for things we have missed the most important thing – a positive relationship with God and those closest to us?

Do you sense God calling you to a deeper, more

An advance on eternity

intimate experience with him than you have ever imagined? His Sabbath peace beckons you. The delight of Sabbath worship calls you. The joy of Sabbath fellowship invites you. Jesus himself gives you a personal invitation to worship him this coming Sabbath.

Come. . . . 'Come to me, all you who are weary and burdened, and I will give you rest.' (Matthew 11:28.)

Why not open your heart to him right now? Why not plead with him to satisfy the inner hunger of the soul? Why not ask him right now to give you a foretaste of eternity this Sabbath? Why not right now ask him to open your eyes to see new beauty in a renewed Sabbath fellowship with him?

─── Chapter six ───
Bible answers to your questions

John was a committed Christian. He and his wife were faithful believers. They wanted to do God's will. As they attended a series of meetings I conducted on Bible prophecy, they were challenged with new truths they had never heard before. Questions loomed large in their minds. The Bible Sabbath particularly troubled them. They were convicted it was truth from the Bible, but their pastor raised some serious questions in their minds. They began to doubt. They seemed confused and needed their questions answered. As we studied the Bible together, their understanding of truth deepened. They found solid answers for their questions. Their doubts disappeared and they discovered the true joy and blessing of Sabbath keeping.

Possibly you, too, have some questions regarding the Bible Sabbath. There may be some Bible passages which are difficult for you to understand. The Bible provides clear answers to our questions. In fact, throughout the Bible our Lord invites us to ask questions and he provides solid answers in his Word.

Jesus declared, 'Sanctify them in the truth; your word is truth.' (John 17:17, NRSV.) Peter adds, 'But in your hearts sanctify Christ as Lord. Always be ready to make your defence to anyone who demands from you an accounting for the hope that is in you; yet do it with gentleness and reverence.' (1 Peter 3:15, NRSV.)

The apostle Paul counsels Timothy in 'rightly

Bible answers to your questions

explaining the word of truth' (2 Timothy 2:15, NRSV).
Isaiah the Old Testament prophet asks, 'Whom will he
teach knowledge, ... ? For it is precept upon precept, .
. . line upon line,' (Isaiah 28:9, 10, NRSV). In other
words, be sure to see the scope of the Bible's teaching
on a particular topic. Do not build your understanding
on one obscure text. If you truly want to understand
what the Bible says on a particular topic, study that
topic from Genesis to Revelation. Let the Holy Spirit
speak to your mind throughout the teachings of
Scripture.

Ask yourself, where is the weight of evidence on this
topic? What do the majority of passages teach? Never
let something which is not as clear to you overshadow
what is clear. If there is a text you do not understand,
let the plain passages in the Bible explain it. Do not
disregard texts and passages of Scripture which are
abundantly plain to cling to something that is not as
clear, simply to defend a doctrine you have previously
been taught.

Here are four principles in discovering truth.

1. Approach the Bible with an open mind, willing to do
   whatever Christ asks you. (John 7:17.)
2. Ask God to send his Holy Spirit to your mind to
   reveal truth. (Matthew 7:7; John 16:13.)
3. Compare each relevant passage of Scripture on a
   given topic. (1 Corinthians 2:13.)
4. Act on the truth God reveals and he will reveal more
   truth. Do not wait to know all the truth to act on the
   truth you know. (John 12:35.)

As we approach his Word with sincere hearts, he will
reveal his truth. He will enlighten our minds. He will
impress us by his Holy Spirit.

You may have questions, but God has answers. As
you read through some of the most commonly asked
questions below and the biblical answers I have
provided, pray God will give you wisdom and

When **God** said
REMEMBER

understanding.

You are not alone in your search for truth. Tens of thousands of others have asked similar questions and found solid answers in God's Word, so read on.

Commonly asked questions regarding the law of God

Didn't Jesus come to do away with the Ten Commandments and establish a new commandment of love? What about Matthew 22:37-40: 'Love God with all your heart and your neighbours as yourself?' Isn't love to God and our neighbours all Jesus requires? These are the new commandments.

It may surprise you to discover the Jesus was summarising the law as given in the Old Testament. Deuteronomy 6:5 declares, 'Love the LORD your God with all your heart.' Leviticus 19:18 adds, 'Love your neighbour as yourself.' The God of the Old Testament is a God of everlasting love (Jeremiah 31:3). In Matthew 22:40, Jesus declared, 'On these two commandments [love to God and our fellow man] hang all the law and the prophets.' (NRSV.) The first four commandments reveal how human beings tangibly demonstrate their love to God. The last six commandments show how they demonstrate their love to their fellow man. Jesus did not come to destroy the law but to fulfil it (Matthew 5:17). He revealed how to keep the law lovingly. He came to magnify the meaning of the law (Isaiah 42:21). Jesus reveals how love is the fulfilling of the law (Romans 13:10). He adds, 'If you love me, you will keep my commandments.' (John 14:15, NRSV.)

Does Paul teach that Christians saved by faith do not have to keep the law?

Paul teaches that Christians are saved not by faith, but by grace through faith. Faith is the hand that takes the salvation freely offered by Jesus. Faith does not lead to disobedience but to obedience. Paul states in no uncertain terms: 'Do we, then, nullify the law by this faith? Not at all!' (Romans 3:31.) Romans 6:1, 2 adds, 'Shall we continue in sin [break the law], that grace may abound? God forbid.' (KJV.)

Is it true that in the Old Testament people were saved by keeping the law, while in the New Testament salvation is by grace?

In both the Old and New Testaments, salvation is by grace through faith. God does not have two methods of salvation. Titus 2:11 affirms, 'For the grace of God that brings salvation has appeared to *all* men.' (Italics supplied.) In the Old Testament, men and women were saved by the Christ who was to come. Each lamb sacrificed pointed forward to the coming of the Messiah (Genesis 3:21; 22:9-13). In the New Testament, men and women are saved by the Christ who has come. In one instance faith looked backward to the Cross. Jesus is the only means of salvation (Acts 4:12).

Since we are under the New Covenant, is it really necessary to keep God's law?

The New Covenant is actually older than the Old Covenant. It was given by God himself in the Garden of Eden when he promised that the Messiah would come to break the deadly hold of Satan upon the human race. The New Covenant contains the promise of redemption from sin through Jesus Christ. He saves us! He writes the principles of the law in our hearts. Love becomes the motivation for obedience. There is a new power in the life (Hebrews 8:10; Ezekiel 36:26; Psalm 40:8). Under the Old Covenant, Israel promised to obey God's commandments in their own strength. They declared, 'We will do everything the LORD has said.' (Exodus 19:8; 24:3, 7.) All attempts at external conformity to God's law lead to frustrated defeat. The law which we cannot keep in our own strength

condemns us (Romans 3:23; 6:23). Under the New Covenant, we belong to a new master – Jesus Christ. We have a new heart and a new standing before God (John 1:12; 2 Corinthians 5:17; Romans 8:1).

Since Paul declares, 'Let no one judge you regarding the Bible Sabbath' (see Colossians 2:16, 17), isn't Sabbath-keeping unnecessary?

This passage, Colossians 2:16, 17, is one of the most misunderstood passages in the Bible. One principle of Bible interpretation is that you do not allow what might be somewhat unclear to keep you from doing what you understand. The Bible teaching on the Sabbath is plain. It was given at Creation (Genesis 2:1-3). Jesus observed it (Luke 4:16). Paul observed it (Acts 13:42-44) and it will be observed in Heaven (Isaiah 66:22, 23). The Bible mentions two kinds of Sabbaths. The seventh-day Sabbath and the yearly Sabbaths. The seventh day Sabbath, instituted at Creation and part of the ten commandment law, is a weekly reminder of the loving, all-powerful Creator. The yearly Sabbath relates specifically to the history of Israel. Colossians 2:16, 17 specifically states: 'Let no one judge you . . . regarding . . . sabbaths, which are a shadow of things to come.' (NKJV.) Hebrews 10:1 connects the law of shadows with animal sacrifice. Ezekiel 45:17 uses the exact same expressions in the exact same order as Colossians 2:16, 17 and connects it all with the ceremonial systems of feasts and sacrifices (meat offerings, drink offerings, feasts, new moons and Sabbaths) to make reconciliation for the house of Israel. Leviticus 23:5-32 discusses the ceremonial Sabbaths: Passover, verse 5; Unleavened Bread, verse 6; Wave Sheaf, verse 10; Firstfruits, verse 17; Trumpets, verse 24; Tabernacles, verse 34; and the Day of Atonement, verse 27-32; are specifically called Sabbaths. These annual Sabbaths were intimately connected to events foreshadowing Christ's death and

Bible answers to your questions

his Second Coming. They were designed by God to be shadows or pointers to the coming Messiah. Leviticus 23:37 uses the language of Colossians 2:16, 17 to describe these ceremonial Sabbaths. Leviticus 23:38 distinguishes the ceremonial Sabbaths from the seventh-day Sabbaths by using the expression 'Besides the Sabbaths of the Lord.' (NKJV.) Since Christ has come, the shadowy Sabbaths of the ceremonial law have found their fulfilment in him. The seventh-day Sabbath continues to lead us back to the Creator God who made us. God's people will keep it as a distinguishing sign of their relationship with him (Revelation 14:12; Ezekiel 20:12, 20).

What about Romans 14:5? 'One man considers one day more sacred than another; another man considers every day alike. Each one should be fully convinced in his own mind.' Really, what difference does a day make?

Sometimes it's helpful to look carefully at what a Bible text does not say as well as what it does say. Verses 5 and 6 say nothing about either worship or the Sabbath. They simply talk about regarding a day. To say this particular day is the Sabbath is an unwarranted assumption. Romans 14:1 sets the tone for the entire passage, indicating that the discussion focuses on 'disputable matters'. Is the seventh-day Sabbath set apart by God at Creation (Genesis 2:1-3) and placed within the heart of the moral law (Exodus 20:8-11) a doubtful matter? Certainly not! The key to our passage is found in verse 6 which states, 'He who observes the day, observes it to the Lord; and he who does not observe the day, to the Lord he does not observe it. He who eats, eats to the Lord, for he gives God thanks; and he who does not eat, to the Lord he does not eat, and gives God thanks.' (NKJV.) The issue revolved around fast days, not Sabbath days. Some Jewish Christians believed there was particular merit in fasting

When God said REMEMBER

on certain days. They judged others by their own standards. The Pharisees fasted at least twice a week and boasted about it (Luke 18:12). In Romans 14, Paul is pointing out that to fast or not to fast on a certain day is a matter of individual conscience, not a matter of God's command.

Didn't the disciples meet on the first day of the week? (See Acts 20:7.)

The reason this meeting is mentioned in the narrative is because Paul was leaving the next day and worked a mighty miracle in raising Eutychus from the dead. It is clear that the meeting is a night meeting. It is the dark part of the first day of the week (Acts 20:7). In Bible times, the dark part of the day preceded the light part (Genesis 1:5). The Sabbath was observed from Friday night at sunset to Saturday night at sunset. (Leviticus 23:32; Mark 1:32.) If this meeting is on the dark part of the first day of the week, it is, in fact, a Saturday night meeting. Paul has met with the believers all Sabbath. He will depart the next day, Sunday, so the meeting continues late into Saturday night. The next day, Sunday, Paul travels by foot to Assos, then sails to Mitylene. The *New English Bible* reading of Acts 20:7 also confirms this as a Saturday night meeting, with Paul travelling on Sunday. If Paul considered Sunday sacred in honour of the resurrection, why would he spend the entire day travelling and not worshipping? The record indicates that Paul was a Sabbath keeper. (See Acts 13:42-44; 17:2; 16:12, 13; 18:4.)

Can we really tell which day the seventh day is?

There are at least four ways in which we can tell for certain that Saturday is the seventh day.
1. The Bible: clearly reveals that Jesus was crucified on the Preparation Day (Luke 23:54). His closest followers rested as commanded on the Sabbath day (Luke 23:56; Mark 16:1). Most Christians recognise

Jesus died on Friday, the Preparation Day; he rested the next day and rose the first day, Sunday. The Sabbath is the day between Friday and Sunday or the seventh day – Saturday.

2. Language: In over 140 languages in the world, the word for the seventh day which we call Saturday is the word *Sabbath*. Language testifies to the Sabbath's preservation through the centuries.

3. Astronomy: The leading astronomers in the world testify to the fact that the weekly cycle has never changed. Centres like the Naval Observatory in the US and the Greenwich Observatory affirm the fact of a constant weekly cycle.

4. History: The Jewish people have kept an accurate record of the Sabbath through the centuries. For over 4,000 years, they have preserved the true Sabbath on Saturday.

I keep Sunday in honour of the resurrection. What's wrong with that? Didn't Jesus rise from the dead on Sunday?

Yes, Jesus certainly rose on Sunday. But he never commanded us to worship in honour of the resurrection. Just as the communion service symbolises his death (1 Corinthians 11:24, 26), baptism symbolises his resurrection (Romans 6:1-6). The symbol of Jesus' resurrection is not worship on the day of the sun adopted into Christianity from pagan Rome's sun worship, but a beautiful ceremony of baptism as a symbol of a new life transformed by the wonder-working power of the Holy Spirit. In baptism by immersion, the old person symbolically dies and is buried, while a new life is resurrected with Christ.

Isn't one day in seven good enough? Why do you put so much emphasis on the Sabbath?

The issue is more than a matter of days. It is a matter of masters. Through a master stroke of

deception, Satan has worked through false religion to change God's law (Daniel 7:25). He has cast the truth to the ground (Daniel 8:12). He has made a break in God's wall of truth. God calls us to repair the breach by keeping his Sabbath (Isaiah 58:12, 13). We ought to obey God rather than men (Acts 5:29). To worship on the seventh day is to accept the authority of your Creator Lord, who commanded the day should be kept (Exodus 20:8-11). To accept knowingly a counterfeit day of worship is to accept an institution initiated and established solely by man in the apostasy. The real question is, then, whose servants are we – God's or man's? (Romans 6:16.) All the celebrations the day before or the day after my birthday do not make these days my birthday. The world's birthday is the Bible Sabbath, the seventh day. It is a memorial to our loving Creator. No other day will do.

Was Peter the first Pope? What did Jesus mean when he said to Peter, 'On this rock I will build my church' (Matthew 16:13-19)?

Caesarea Philippi was a centre of Greek philosophy, Roman logic and Jewish traditional religion. Jesus set himself against the backdrop of the world's great religious and philosophical systems, asking, 'Who do men say I am?' After they answered, 'John the Baptist, Elijah, Jeremiah,' he asked, 'Who do you say I am?' Jesus longed to deepen their faith. He desired to draw out a messianic confession. Peter instantly responded, 'You are the Christ, the Son of the living God.' This thought could be inspired only by the Holy Spirit. Jesus affirmed Peter's faith by declaring, 'You are *Petros* (a movable stone), but upon this rock (this immovable foundation – that I am the Christ) I will build my church and the gates of hell shall not prevail against it.' The Church is built upon Jesus Christ. He is the cornerstone rejected by the builders (1 Peter 2:4-8). Peter clearly understood the rock was Jesus. Paul

Bible answers to your questions

clarifies the issue in 1 Corinthians 10:4 by proclaiming, 'That Rock was Christ.' David declares, 'My soul finds rest in God alone; my salvation comes from him. He alone is my rock and my salvation' (Psalm 62:1, 2). There is no other foundation (1 Corinthians 3:11) except Jesus. The gates of hell will never triumph over his Church. Peter objected against Jesus' going to Jerusalem. The courageous disciple misunderstood Jesus' mission. Jesus said, 'Get behind me, Satan' (meaning Satan was influencing him). No, the Church was not built upon Peter's weakness, but upon Jesus' strength. Peter discovered the marvellous truth for himself. Jesus became the source of his strength, the centre of his life and the foundation upon which he stood.

What are the 'keys of the kingdom' which Jesus gave Peter and the rest of the disciples (Matthew 16:19)?
Keys open and shut doors. Jesus said, 'I am the door.' (John 10:9, NKJV.) 'No man comes to the Father except through me.' (John 14:6.) There is no other name under heaven whereby men may be saved (Acts 4:12). All the Scriptures testify of Jesus (John 5:39). The scribes and Pharisees took away the 'key of knowledge' regarding the Messiah (Luke 11:52). They shut up Heaven. The 'keys' Jesus gave to Peter were his own words, his teachings, regarding how men and women could have forgiveness for sin, freedom from condemnation and peace through his shed blood and death on Calvary's Cross. A knowledge of Jesus, the promised Messiah, opens Heaven (Isaiah 22:22).

—— Chapter seven ——
Keeping the Sabbath wholly

Jonathan was worried. His final exam was scheduled for Sabbath. To take the exam would be a violation of his conscience. He made an appointment with his professor, explained his situation and asked for the opportunity to take the exam on another date. His professor flatly refused. He explained that there were no exceptions. Jonathan had only two options; either take the exam and pass the class or miss it and fail.

Certainly Jonathan did not want to waste the whole semester. He did not relish retaking the whole course. He earnestly prayed God would open the door for him to take the exam some other day than the Sabbath.

As the day of the exam dawned, Jonathan calmly walked to church Sabbath morning, believing God would honour his trust. There are times when God acts powerfully and miraculously to demonstrate his greatness. After the exam, as the professor was walking home from class with the students' exam papers securely in his briefcase, he was robbed. The only thing that was taken was his briefcase. The professor was not harmed but his briefcase with all of the exams was gone forever.

Since graduation was only a few days away, the principal of the school made a surprising announcement. Each student in the class would be awarded a pass in the exam. Their total score for the class would be their test averages up until the time of the exam. Jonathan was overwhelmed with gratitude to

Keeping the Sabbath wholly

the God who heard his prayer and honoured his faith.

God blesses faithfulness

God's promise to his faithful followers in Bible times is just as true today. Our Lord declares, 'Those who honour me I will honour, but those who despise me will be disdained.' (1 Samuel 2:30.) The words of Scripture echo down through the centuries. They speak to us with just as much force today. They are no less true than when they were written millenniums ago. 'All these blessings will come upon you and accompany you if you obey the LORD your God' (Deuteronomy 28:2). God promises his richest blessings to those who obey him. This is especially true of those who are committed to keep his seventh-day Sabbath each week. At Creation God 'blessed the seventh day' (Genesis 2:3). Whatever God blesses is blessed forever (1 Chronicles 17:27). Since God's eternal blessing is in the seventh-day Sabbath, we are richly blessed as we keep it (Isaiah 56:2).

This leads us to some specific questions. How do we keep the Sabbath? Are there some activities which are incompatible with the Sabbath? Are there some things which will destroy our Sabbath blessing? What is God's purpose for the Sabbath?

God does not give us a 'to do' and 'not to do' list of activities for the Sabbath. He does not define each minute detail of Sabbath keeping. He does give us principles of proper Sabbath observance. These principles guide us. They shape our Sabbath experience. As we seek God in prayer, committing our will to him, the Holy Spirit will guide us into a rich experience in Sabbath keeping. We will sense his presence and experience his love each Sabbath.

Let's examine three biblical principles which will guide us in our Sabbath keeping.

Principle 1. The Sabbath is a day dedicated to

worshipping our Creator.

The essence of Sabbath keeping is worship. On Sabbath, with all of Heaven's host, we joyously proclaim, 'You are worthy, our Lord and God, to receive glory and honour and power, for you created all things, and by your will they were created and have their being.' (Revelation 4:11.) We were created by a loving God. Each Sabbath we thank him for the gift of life by worshipping him as Creator. According to Leviticus 23:3, 'There are six days when you may work, but the seventh day is a Sabbath of rest, a day of sacred assembly.' The Sabbath is a sacred assembly of God's people for worship and praise.

Throughout the centuries God's chosen people, the Jews, worshipped him each Sabbath. In the New Testament Jesus gives us a positive example of Sabbath keeping. The gospel writer Luke records Jesus' Sabbath practices this way: 'He went to Nazareth, where he had been brought up, and on the Sabbath day he went into the synagogue, as was his custom. And he stood up to read.' (Luke 4:16.) For Jesus, the Sabbath was a day of fellowship with God in worship. When the people of God meet together to sing praises to his name, study his Word, seek him in prayer and fellowship with one another, they are richly blessed. Jesus left his tools in Joseph's carpenter shop at Nazareth each Sabbath to attend worship in the synagogue. Sabbath worship was important to Jesus. His 'custom' or 'practice' was to praise his heavenly Father, absorb his Word and fellowship with his people each Sabbath.

Sabbath worship was spiritually invigorating for Jesus, and it will refresh us spiritually as well.

New Testament Christians met each Sabbath to renew their spiritual strength. On Sabbath they met together to encourage one another. They followed the counsel of the apostle Paul to the Hebrews when he said, 'And let us consider how we may spur one

Keeping the Sabbath wholly

another on towards love and good deeds. Let us not give up meeting together, as some are in the habit of doing, but let us encourage one another – and all the more as you see the Day approaching.' (Hebrews 10:24, 25.) Each Sabbath God invites us to find our deepest satisfaction in worship. Sabbath is a slice of Heaven. In Heaven's plan, God allows us to experience eternity each week as we enter the joy of Sabbath worship. On Sabbath we place priority on worship, not work. The Sabbath liberates us from the grind of daily toil. On Sabbath we are free from the burden of earning a living to experience life at its best.

The fourth commandment is too plain to be misunderstood. God knew that if he simply gave us good advice, many of us would ignore it, so he gave us a command: 'Remember the Sabbath day, to keep it holy. Six days you shall labour and do all your work, but the seventh day *is* the Sabbath of the LORD your God. *In it* you shall do no work . . .' (Exodus 20:8-10, first part, NKJV, emphasis supplied). God says, 'Remember,' but most of the world has forgotten. The Sabbath is the almost-forgotten commandment. We can only keep holy what God has made holy. No other day can be a substitute for the Sabbath because the Sabbath is the only day God made holy. We keep it holy by giving him our deepest allegiance in Sabbath worship. To place priority on work rather than worship defiles the day God made holy and dishonours God.

Jesus said, 'Then you will know the truth, and the truth will set you free.' (John 8:32.) The truth about Sabbath worship liberates us from the unceasing burden of continued work. Every Sabbath we are reminded by an all-powerful God and loving Creator that our intrinsic worth does not depend on how much we accomplish. We are called from work to worship.

Millions of people find their identity in what they do. Their work defines them. The Sabbath invites us to find our true worth, not in what we do, but in who we are.

When God said
REMEMBER

The Sabbath is a weekly reminder, pointing us to learn of our eternal value in God's sight.

The French Revolution

During the godless French Revolution, with the dawning of the so-called Age of Reason, the French adopted what they termed 'The French Republican Calendar' or 'French Revolutionary Calendar'. This calendar was used by the French for twelve years from 1793 to 1805. It eradicated the seven-day weekly cycle, abolished worship and created a ten-day week. All workers worked nine days and on the tenth had a day of rest and merriment.

Napoleon abolished this French Revolutionary Calendar with its ten-day week and demanded France return to the seven-day weekly cycle. French workers were not faring well at all under this new calendar with nine days of work and one day of rest. There is a natural rhythm in the weekly cycle which leads us to worship our Creator. To ignore Eden's weekly cycle given at Creation simply makes us vulnerable to physical, mental and emotional breakdowns. God created us for himself. We were made as worshipping beings. A commitment to keep the Sabbath holy makes an enormous difference in our lives.

As I have travelled to more than seventy countries, sharing Jesus and the Gospel of his grace, I have seen thousands take a stand to follow him and keep his Sabbath holy. Some of these people have experienced a real test to keep the Sabbath. Many have been threatened with the loss of their jobs. Their employers have bluntly told them that if they failed to show up for work on Sabbath they would be fired. Time after time I have seen God work miracles.

Sabbath-keeping experiences

Sandra was a postal worker. Although she had seniority her supervisor threatened her with the loss of

Keeping the Sabbath wholly

her job if she did not work on Sabbath. We entered into earnest prayer for Sandra. We claimed Christ's promise in Matthew 6:33, 34 (first part): 'But seek first his kingdom and his righteousness, and all these things will be given to you as well. Therefore do not worry about tomorrow.' Miraculously, Sandra's supervisor reversed his initial decision. She kept her job and got Sabbaths off.

Roger shut down his retail store on Sabbath. Since he did nearly 30% of his business on that day, his friends felt he was crazy. They really thought he'd lost his mind. He placed a sign in the store window which read, 'Closed for the Bible Sabbath'. The first few weeks were rough. Sales were down but surprisingly they gradually climbed. Roger claimed God's promise. 'My God will meet all your needs according to his glorious riches in Christ Jesus.' (Philippians 4:19.) He found God to be faithful. The issue regarding Sabbath work is one of trust. Do we trust God enough to put our lives fully in his hands? Do we believe he will care for us if we are faithful to him?

The decision not to work on the Sabbath any longer is extremely difficult for many people. We have our mortgages, rent, car payments, credit card bills, and a host of other expenses which need to be paid. God does not always get us a better, higher paying job, but when we decide to be faithful to him he does always meet our needs. He does always bless our lives. He does always fill us with an inner sense of contentment when we do what is right. The honour of his throne is behind the promises he has made. Since it is 'impossible for God to lie' (Hebrews 6:18), we can be absolutely certain he will take the responsibility to provide us with the necessities of life if we are faithful to him.

Sabbath worship is essential for a healthy spiritual life. If we are going to grow in Christ, weekly Sabbath worship is vital.

When **God** said
REMEMBER

Principle 2. The Sabbath is a day exclusively set apart for physical, mental and spiritual renewal.

The Israelites drifted away from God when they defiled the Sabbath. In the days of Nehemiah the prophet, the common activities of life crowded out the sacredness of the Sabbath. The Israelites were influenced by their heathen neighbours. Nehemiah describes the scene this way. 'In those days I saw men in Judah treading winepresses on the Sabbath and bringing in grain and loading it on donkeys, together with wine, grapes, figs and all other kinds of loads. And they were bringing all this into Jerusalem on the Sabbath. Therefore I warned them against selling food on that day.' (Nehemiah 13:15.)

Nehemiah was concerned. God's Sabbath had become a common, ordinary day. The day our Creator set aside for spiritual, physical and mental renewal became a day of exhausting toil. The day of liberation from the bondage of buying and selling, working and earning deteriorated into a business-as-usual day. Nehemiah could not keep silent. His words echoed like thunder through the streets of Jerusalem. 'I rebuked the nobles of Judah and said to them, What is this wicked thing you are doing – desecrating the Sabbath day?' (Nehemiah 13:17.) The principle is plain. When we become so absorbed in the earthly that we forget the eternal, we defile the Sabbath. The book of Isaiah adds this insight; 'If you keep your feet from breaking the Sabbath and from doing as you please on my holy day, if you call the Sabbath a delight and the LORD's holy day honourable, and if you honour it by not going your own way and not doing as you please or speaking idle words, then you will find your joy in the LORD, and I will cause you to ride on the heights of the land. . . .' (Isaiah 58:13, 14.) In other words, we shall be abundantly blessed.

Keeping the Sabbath wholly

A personal testimony

When I became a Christian, I was playing basketball on a high school sports team in Norwich, Connecticut. Our team qualified for the New England championship. This was an exciting thing for a group of teenage boys from a small town. The tournament was scheduled from Thursday to Sunday in Springfield, Massachusetts, which meant playing basketball all day Sabbath and, of course, missing worship. I had recently begun to understand the significance of the Bible Sabbath and attend church on Sabbath. For me to break the Sabbath was to be disobedient to Christ. The Sabbath was a symbol of my allegiance to the God I served. I faced a tough decision. The decision was extremely difficult. Should I stay home and keep the Sabbath or travel with the basketball team and do what I naturally wanted to do? My mind began to rationalise. What's wrong with playing just this one time? But deep within the fabric of my being I knew travelling to the basketball tournament and disregarding the Sabbath as the Lord's Day would be a violation of my conscience.

I wanted to go badly, but one question continued to echo in my mind. What is more important, basketball or Jesus? In my anguish I called a godly Christian woman who had become sort of a spiritual mentor. This woman of faith was a diligent Bible student. When I asked her for her counsel she put it in very simple terms; 'Mark, be faithful to Jesus.' Based on her advice and my inner conviction, I made a decision not to go to the tournament. It seemed that I had just ruined my chances to travel, sleep in a hotel, eat in restaurants and see the world.

As I look back on this experience I have to smile. Today I have had the opportunity to travel to countries around the world, sharing God's Gospel of grace. I have had the indescribable thrill of seeing people come

to Christ from Montreal to Moscow, from Russia to Rwanda, from Chile to China. God has immeasurably enriched my life since I made that initial commitment. Giving up my dreams enabled me to follow God's dreams for my life. We may think that we are making great sacrifices to follow God but he gives us much more in return. The apostle Peter said to Jesus, 'We have left everything to follow you!' (Mark 10:28.) You can almost hear Peter wondering aloud, 'What will we receive in return?' Jesus gives Peter a remarkable response; 'I tell you the truth, Jesus replied, no-one who has left home or brothers or sisters or mother or father or children or fields for me and the gospel will fail to receive a hundred times as much in this present age (homes, brothers, sisters, mothers, children and fields – and with them, persecutions) and in the age to come, eternal life.' (Mark 10:29, 30.) In other words, Jesus says, 'Yes, there will be challenges if you commit your life to me, but whatever you give up I will give you one hundred times more in blessings.' When we make a decision to follow Jesus, he pledges to meet our needs and to fill our lives with joy, peace, forgiveness, power, contentment, satisfaction and purpose. I can certainly testify that God faithfully fulfils his word.

One of the great blessings God gives us is Sabbath rest. How can we put a price on the renewed physical, mental and spiritual rest Jesus gives us as we keep his Sabbath. I cannot put a value on the blessing of God's Sabbath to me. Believe me, this time of spiritual rest is an essential part of my life. It keeps me going in my hectic schedule. It has helped to strengthen my bond with my family. This leads to the third great biblical principle regarding the Sabbath.

Principle 3. The Sabbath is a day of building closer relationships with our family and friends and blessing those around us in service.

Let your mind drift back over the millenniums to the

Keeping the Sabbath wholly

beauty and magnificence of Eden. On the sixth day God created Adam and Eve. The Bible records, 'God saw all that he had made, and it was very good.' (Genesis 1:31.) There was no sin, sickness, suffering or death in the splendour of that garden. Since God is love and we are created to love, God gave to our first parents a gift of love – the Sabbath (1 John 4:8; Genesis 2:1-3). The first complete day Adam and Eve spent together was the Sabbath. Their first intimate moments of sharing and communicating were on the Sabbath. Sabbath is a day for strengthening relationships. It gives us time for our loving heavenly Father and one another. The Sabbath is a day to get to know one another better. It is a day to give time to strengthening our relationship with God and those we love.

Do you ever feel the week just rushes by and time for family is crowded out? Some studies indicate that fathers spend less than two hours a week one-on-one with their children. The Sabbath reminds us every week of what is really important.

The Jewish playwright, Herman Wouk, would not be without the Sabbath in his life. He describes how the Sabbath is an island of peace in the chaos of Broadway society.

At sundown Friday night, he leaves the stress of the littered theatre with the frenzy of opening night just hours away. As he arrives home to the warm embrace of his wife and the smiles of his children, he is encircled in loving relationships. The candles are lighted. The table is set. The family eats and shares together. The children ask questions and the world of show business is forgotten.

When Wouk returns to the theatre Saturday evening after sunset, nothing much has changed there, *but he has changed*. His relaxing, restorative Sabbath has drawn him closer to his God and his family.

A colleague remarked to Wouk after he came back

to the theatre one Saturday night, 'I don't envy your religion but I do envy your Sabbath.' Who would not want to spend a day building better relationships with those you love?

For Jesus, Sabbath was about loving relationships. It was about service. This is precisely why Jesus performed numerous miracles on the Sabbath. On Sabbath Jesus revealed the Father's compassion to suffering humanity. When the Jewish religious leaders criticised Jesus for performing acts of healing on the Sabbath, he commented, 'It is lawful to do good on the Sabbath.' (Matthew 12:12.) The Sabbath is a day for doing good. Is a neighbour sick? Bring her a hot bowl of delicious homemade soup. Have you heard about friends who are discouraged? Call them on the phone to lift their spirits. Do you sense the widower down the street is lonely? Invite him over for lunch.

On Sabbath we remember our Creator. There is no better place to do that than out in nature. For years my wife and I spent many Sabbath afternoons hiking when our children were growing up. Even now, although our children are grown and married, my wife and I often spend Sabbaths in nature. We enjoy sharing together in the beauties of nature. Walking the trails near our home, listening to the bird songs, seeing an occasional deer, smelling the fragrant aroma of the wild flowers, relaxes our tired bodies and lifts our spirits for another week.

The Sabbath is not drudgery. It is life-giving. The Sabbath is not a burden. It is a blessing. The Sabbath is much more than a duty. It is a delight.

If you have not experienced the exhilarating joy of Sabbath worship, why not begin this week? It you have not entered into the peace of 'Sabbath rest', why not start now? If you would like a closer relationship with your loved ones and friends, the Sabbath experience awaits you. The Sabbath is not simply something to be debated; it is a joy to be experienced. Why not

Keeping the Sabbath wholly

experience the blessings of Sabbath for yourself? With arms wide open Jesus says, 'Come to me, all you who are weary and burdened, and I will give you rest.'

When **God** said
REMEMBER

--- Chapter eight ---

Delusions

David Copperfield is one of the greatest illusionists of all time. He performs more than 500 shows each year around the world. His illusions have included making the Statue of Liberty disappear, levitating over the Grand Canyon and walking through the Great Wall of China. Over a two-year period he reportedly made in the region of £100 million. Evidently people will pay a whole lot of money to be deceived. But David Copperfield does not hold a candle to the universe's greatest deceiver. Satan is the master illusionist. He is 'a liar and the father of lies' (John 8:44). In Heaven's perfect environment he deceived one third of all of the angels (Revelation 12:9). In Eden, he deceived Eve, then Adam. Throughout the millenniums the evil one has used his deceptive delusions to lead millions astray. His greatest delusion is illusion. He makes things appear to be true that are not.

His greatest deceptions are religious ones. The devil takes falsehood and clothes it in the garb of truth. He confuses the mind by cleverly disguising pagan practices in religious garments.

The Bible's last book, Revelation, unmasks the plans of the devil. It reveals his delusions.

This is especially true in the symbolism of Revelation's two women – the woman in white described in Revelation 12 and the woman in scarlet portrayed in Revelation 17. Nowhere in Revelation are truth and error brought into such sharp contrast as in

Delusions

these two chapters. In the symbols of the woman in white and the woman in scarlet, John graphically portrays two systems of religion – truth and falsehood. The woman in white 'keeps the commandments of God' (Revelation 12:17, NRSV). The woman in scarlet is 'holding in her hand a golden cup'. The gold of the cup deceives men and women with respect to the matter of its contents. The cup which appears so magnificent is filled with 'abominations' (Revelation 17:4, NRSV). Abomination is another way of expressing rebellion or lawlessness. While the woman in white of Revelation 12 leads her followers to obedience to God's commandments, the woman in scarlet passes around an illusion of truth in a cup of falsehoods leading to disobedience.

The fundamental issue is God's way or man's way and, as we shall see in this chapter, the Sabbath is at the very heart of this end-time controversy.

The book of Revelation describes the Church as a pure woman. Christ is her husband; the Church is his bride. Christ, the head of the Church, gives guidance and direction to his bride. The Bible pictures the true Church as a pure woman – one faithful to her husband, one who has not committed spiritual adultery. The false church is represented in the Bible by a harlot, or an adulteress, who has left her true lover, Jesus Christ, and united with the world.

John the Revelator describes one of the most significant moments in human history: 'A great and wondrous sign appeared in heaven: a woman clothed with the sun, with the moon under her feet and a crown of twelve stars on her head. She was pregnant and cried out in pain as she was about to give birth.' (Revelation 12:1, 2.)

According to Scripture, this child was to rule all nations. Ultimately, he was 'snatched up to God and to his throne' (verse 5). Obviously, this is a description of Jesus.

The Bible says this woman stands on the moon. As the moon reflects the glory of the sun, so the Old Testament Church reflects the glory of the Gospel which blazed forth in Jesus. When the Old Testament scene faded, the New Testament Church, clothed with the glory of Christ, arose in splendour. The garland of the twelve stars on the woman's head signifies that the New Testament Church would be guided by divinely inspired apostles. This is a picture of God's true Church, clothed with the righteousness of Christ and anchored in Scripture. The pure, true Church, unadulterated by human traditions, untouched by human doctrine, based on the Word of God. Yet the picture dramatically changes in the seventeenth chapter of Revelation.

'Then the angel carried me away in the Spirit into a desert. There I saw a woman sitting on a scarlet beast that was covered with blasphemous names and had seven heads and ten horns. The woman was dressed in purple and scarlet, and was glittering with gold, precious stones and pearls. She held a golden cup in her hand, filled with abominable things and the filth of her adulteries.' (Revelation 17:3-4.)

This bejewelled woman passes around the wine cup of her false doctrines and the world becomes drunk. She is a harlot. She has left her true lover Jesus Christ. In Revelation chapter 12 the apostle John describes the true Church. In Revelation chapter 17 he describes the false church system. This corrupted woman is the 'mother of prostitutes'. In other words, she has many daughters or churches which have become drunk with the wine of her false doctrine and have also been led astray.

The story of these two women – one dressed in white and the other in purple and scarlet – is the amazing saga of the controversy between good and evil, truth and error, God's Word and human tradition.

Delusions

The woman in white

The Bible teaches that there are two great systems of religion. One is centred in Jesus, who is 'the way, the truth, and the life' (John 14:6). It is based solidly on the teachings of Scripture. Consequently, in Revelation 12 the true Church is pictured as a woman in white. Her doctrines are pure; she is loyal to her true Master. She has not compromised the truth. God is looking for a Church that does not mingle truth and error. He is looking for a people who are living in harmony with the truth of his Word. The woman in white of Revelation 12 represents God's true, visible Church on Earth, his faithful people through the ages who have not compromised Bible doctrine.

The woman in scarlet

In addition to the woman in white, the Bible also describes a woman in scarlet with a cup of wine in her hand, representing false doctrine. She is the great blasphemous mother Church, and many churches have drunk of her wine. The Bible says that she rides upon a scarlet-coloured beast. In the Bible, a beast represents a political system (Daniel 7:17, 23).

This false church, adorned in scarlet and purple colours, is the mother of prostitutes. She has left her true lover, Jesus, by placing human traditions and the decrees of church councils above the Word of God. She is an adulteress in the sense that she has betrayed scriptural teachings. She is the great mother church, and along with her are other churches who have also left the true biblical doctrines.

Notice Revelation 17:5: 'This title was written on her forehead: MYSTERY, BABYLON THE GREAT, THE MOTHER OF PROSTITUTES AND OF THE ABOMINATIONS OF THE EARTH.' To understand Revelation chapter 17, we must first understand this expression, 'Mystery, Babylon the Great'. The fallen church system of Revelation 17 has teachings and

doctrines which are very similar to the pagan teachings of Old Testament Babylon. In the Old Testament the people of God – Israel – were in constant conflict with the opposing forces of Babylon. God's true church was the nation of Israel. In New Testament times, the Christian Church becomes spiritual Israel. (Galatians 3:29.) The woman in white represents true spiritual Israel, Christ's true followers. Individuals of every nationality who accept Jesus and his doctrines become his true followers. They become his chosen people, just as Israel was in Old Testament times.

In the Old Testament, the kingdom of Babylon established a counterfeit system of worship. In the same way, spiritual Babylon represents counterfeit worship. Spiritual Babylon continues the principles of Old Testament literal Babylon in its religious observances.

Characteristics of spiritual Babylon

Who is this woman in scarlet? What are these Old Testament Babylonian principles she duplicates? Revelation 17:2 describes her as committing fornication with the kings of the earth. 'The inhabitants of the earth were made drunk with the wine of her fornication' (verse 2, NKJV). Therefore, Revelation's picture of a woman on a scarlet-coloured beast represents a union of Church and state. The emphasis here is the dominance of the Church over political powers. The scarlet woman (the fallen church system) rides or dominates the beast (state powers).

The Bible shows that there are two basic systems of religion: the true system outlined in Revelation 12, and the false system outlined in Revelation 17. It is true that not everyone in the true Church will be saved. There are some in it who do not have a heart experience with Jesus. A denominational label does not save any individual. The Bible also says that there are many in the false church who know Jesus and love him but who

Delusions

do not know all the truth. God is attempting to lead every man, woman and child from the false system to the true system.

Babylon began with the Tower of Babel. It was there that God confused their languages. The city of Babylon was later built over the site. The name *Babylon* sounds like the Hebrew word for confusion, recalling the confusion of languages at Babel.

Commenting on the symbolic woman, Babylon, who rides on the scarlet beast, Robert Jamieson, A. R. Fausset and David Brown say in their *Bible Commentary*: 'State and Church are precious gifts of God. But the State being desecrated . . . becomes *beastlike*; the Church apostatizing becomes the *harlot*' (page 593, emphasis supplied).

Babylon – a human system

Let's go back to the Old Testament and look at five identifying features of Babylon there. In Genesis 10:8-10, the Bible describes the origin of the city of Babylon. 'Cush became the father of Nimrod; he was the first on earth to become a mighty warrior. He was a mighty hunter before the Lord. . . . The beginning of his kingdom was Babel' (NRSV). The founder of Babel (later called Babylon) was a rebel against God who led out in establishing a system contrary to God.

In the days of Daniel, Nebuchadnezzar boastfully claimed, 'Is not this the great Babylon I have built as the royal residence, by my mighty power and for the glory of my majesty?' (Daniel 4:30.) As Lucifer before him, Nebuchadnezzar had 'I' trouble. Spiritual Babylon is a man-made system of religion with an earthly, human leader substituting his headship for the headship of Christ.

The true Church of God directs men and women to Jesus Christ as its only head. The false system directs men and women to human spiritual leaders rather than to Jesus alone as our great High Priest. Speaking of

Jesus, the Bible says, 'He is the head of the body, the church; he is the beginning and the firstborn from among the dead, so that in everything he might have the supremacy.' (Colossians 1:18.)

The Bible says that the true Church of God does not have an earthly head but, rather, a heavenly one. The true Church of God points men and women to Jesus, who can forgive their sins and release them from the bondage of sin. Revelation's spiritual Babylon is an earthly system of religion based on human tradition with a human leader.

Let's summarise. The first two characteristics of the false religious system of Babylon are: (1) accepting tradition above the truths of God's Word and (2) having a human, earthly head of the Church rather than Christ.

Babylon – a system centred in image worship

Let's notice a third characteristic of ancient Babylon: Babylon is the source of idolatry.

It is only as we understand ancient Babylon in the Old Testament that we can understand who spiritual Babylon is and God's call to come out of her. Dr Alexander Hislop states: 'Babylon was the primal source from which all these systems of idolatry flowed' (*The Two Babylons*, page 12). In the Old Testament, Babylon was a centre of image worship. The great temples of Babylon were filled with images of the Babylonian gods before which pagan worshippers bowed in reverence. God's sanctuary at Jerusalem had no such images. In the New Testament Christian Church, individuals were instructed to worship Christ directly. There was to be no worship through images.

The Bible plainly states: 'You shall not make for yourself an idol in the form of anything in heaven above or on the earth beneath or in the waters below. You shall not bow down to them or worship them' (Exodus 20:4, 5).

Delusions

The Scripture instruction is plain. If images are introduced into worship, it is highly likely that the image will be considered sacred and receive the homage due to God alone. History testifies that this has happened repeatedly. Images have been reverenced and kissed; relics have been considered holy; statues are embraced almost as gods.

Babylon – ancestor worship

There is a fourth identifying feature of ancient Babylon that also applies to spiritual Babylon: the concept of an immortal soul that lives on after death. In Ezekiel 8:13 the Bible says, 'Again, he said, You will see them doing things that are even more detestable.' (More detestable, that is, than worshipping idols.) Verse 14 adds, 'Then he brought me to the entrance to the north gate of the house of the LORD, and I saw women sitting there, mourning for Tammuz.'

Who was Tammuz and why were the women weeping?

Tammuz was the Babylonian god of vegetation. The Babylonians believed that when spring gave way to summer and the summer heat scorched the crops, Tammuz died. Therefore, they wept and prayed that he might return from the underworld. The concept of the immortal soul does not come from the Bible. It slipped into the Christian Church through Babylonian beliefs. Its roots are in Babylon, yet the doctrine was fully developed in Greek philosophy. The following quotations clearly describe the origin of the pagan doctrine of immortality. The first is from Amos Phelps, a nineteenth-century Methodist minister:

'This doctrine can be traced through the muddy channels of a corrupted Christianity, a perverted Judaism, a pagan philosophy, a superstitious idolatry, to the great instigator of mischief in the Garden of Eden. The Protestants borrowed it from the Catholics, the Catholics from the Pharisees, the Pharisees from

the pagans, and the pagans from the old Serpent, who first preached the doctrine amid the lowly bowels of Paradise to an audience all too willing to hear and heed the new and fascinating theology – "Ye shall not surely die". ' (Amos Phelps, *Is Man by Nature Immortal?*)

The Bible is very plain about what happens to people when they die:

'For the wages of sin is death, but the gift of God is eternal life in Christ Jesus our Lord.' (Romans 6:23.)

'When their breath departs, they return to the earth; on that very day their plans perish.' (Psalm 146:4, NRSV.)

'For the living know that they will die, but the dead know nothing.' (Ecclesiastes 9:5.)

The *Authorised Version* of the Bible uses the word *soul* approximately sixteen hundred times, but it never once uses the expression *immortal soul*. Repeatedly Scripture affirms that only God has immortality (see 1 Timothy 6:16). It was the Babylonians who held the concept that an immortal soul left the body at death. Therefore, the Babylonians established a system of gods and goddesses, worshipping the spirits of those who supposedly lived on. God's people, the Israelites, had a totally different belief. They taught that when people died, their breath went forth, they returned to the earth, and in that very day their thoughts perished.

Revelation describes two great systems of religion. The true system, referred to in Revelation 12, is based on the Word of God, with the pure doctrines of his Word leading men and women to trust Jesus alone. It leads them to understand that they are to come to Christ and worship him directly, without images. It leads them to understand that when people die they sleep until the resurrection. It affirms the biblical truth that the soul is not some conscious entity that lives on endlessly in the spirit world after death.

Revelation 17 describes a false religious system it refers to as Babylon the Great, the apostate mother church. This church is based, not on the Word of God,

Delusions

but on tradition. It has an earthly head that claims to take the place of Christ. It teaches that when people die they do not sleep until the resurrection, but rather have immortal souls that live on after death. It passes its false wine cup around so that other churches drink the wine of false doctrine of this mother church. They, too, accept the false idea that the soul lives on after death – outside of and independent of the body.

Babylon – the centre of sun worship

A fifth characteristic of Babylon, both in the Old Testament and in the New, is mentioned in Ezekiel 8:16. This is, in fact, the key principle defining Babylon:

'He then brought me into the inner court of the house of the LORD, and there at the entrance to the temple, between the portico and the altar, were about twenty-five men. With their backs towards the temple of the LORD and their faces towards the east, they were bowing down to the sun in the east.'

The prophet Ezekiel saw these men following the Babylonian practice of sun worship. Turning their faces towards the east, they knelt and worshipped the sun god as the sun rose in the eastern sky. Ancient Babylonian calendars, with the sun at the centre, reveal the importance the Babylonians placed on sun worship. The Babylonians did not believe that they were fashioned by the hands of a loving Creator. They believed the sun, the largest luminous body in the heavens, was the source of life. In adoration, they bowed to worship it.

Down through the millenniums false worship was often rooted in sun worship. Satan exalted the object of Creation above the Creator. The Assyrians worshipped the sun god Shamash. The Egyptians worshipped the sun god Amon Ra. The Hittites worshipped Arinna the sun goddess. The Konarak sun wheel is famous throughout India. The Nordic Trundholm sun chariot symbolised the sun worship of the Vikings. Helios of

Greece and Mithra of Persia and Rome were worshipped as sun gods by multitudes. The Sabbath called God's people to worship their Creator. Sun worship beckoned them to worship an object of Creation.

The first and second century Christian Church in Rome was largely composed of Gentile Christians. This is quite different from the Church in Jerusalem and the Middle East, which was largely a Jewish/Christian Church.

The New Schaff-Herzog Encyclopaedia of Religious Knowledge, vol. 7, page 421, makes this startling observation: 'In the first Christian century there were organized at Rome associations of the followers of Mithra. Among the Romans the sun god Mithra was known by the masses as "Sol Invictus – the Invisible Sun". The Emperor Aurelian's mother was a priestess of the sun. The emperor himself was especially devoted to sun worship. His biographer, Flavius Vopiscus, states that the emperor officially proclaimed the solar deity as "Sol Dominus Imperii Romani" (The Sun, Lord of the Roman Empire).'

Well-known historian Arthur Weigall in his book, *Paganism in our Christianity*, page 145, states, 'As a solar festival, Sunday was the sacred day of Mithra; and it is interesting to notice that since Mithra was addressed as "Dominus Lord", Sunday must have been the Lord's Day long before Christian times.' He makes a telling point. Since Sunday was the day dedicated to the pagan god Mithra and since Mithra was considered to be 'Lord', Sunday was considered the Lord's day not of Christ originally but of a pagan god.

The *Catholic Encyclopaedia* adds this insight: 'Sunday was kept holy in honour of Mithra' (vol. 10, pages 403, 404, article *Mithraism*). Scholar Franz Cumont adds, 'The dies Solis (Sunday) was evidently the most sacred of the week for the faithful of Mithra

Delusions

and like the Christians they had to keep the Sunday holy and not the Sabbath' (F. Cumont, *Textes et Monuments Figurés Relatifs aux Mystères de Mithra*, vol. 1, page 119).

Professor Agostinho de Almeida Paiva in his outstanding book on Mithraism rounds out the story this way: 'The first day of each week, Sunday, was consecrated to Mithra since times remote as several authors affirm. Because the sun was god, the Lord par excellence, Sunday came to be called the Lord's Day, as later was done by Christianity' (*Mithraism*, page 3).

The evidence is undeniable. Gentiles converting to Christianity in Rome were influenced by Mithraism – sun worship. They already had a sense that Sunday was the Lord's Day since they believed Mithra or Helios (the sun) was the Lord. It would not be difficult for those Gentile Christians to shift their allegiance to Jesus rather than Mithra on the sun's day.

When Constantine became the emperor of the Roman Empire, he chose as his family god Apollo – the sun god – identified with the old Roman Sol since the time of the Caesars.

With an anti-Jewish sentiment rising in the empire, social and political discord flourishing and corrupt church leaders grasping for power, Sunday became the vehicle to unite the empire.

The pagan Roman Emperor, recently converted to Christianity, was urged by church leaders to promote a common day of worship on Sunday to advance the power of the Church.

Constantine himself, in a letter addressed to Alexander, Bishop of Alexandria (AD313-325), clearly states his religious policy for the Roman Empire in these words: 'My design was, first, to bring the diverse judgements formed by all nations respecting the deity in a condition as it were of settled uniformity . . .' (*The Life of Constantine*, book 2, chapter 65).

In passing his six civil Sunday laws, Constantine

hoped to unite his empire. He wisely realised that one way to do this was a common day of rest, festivity and worship throughout the empire. A day that both pagans and Christians could agree upon. A. P. Stanley in his *History of the Eastern Church* writes: 'The retention of the old pagan name of "dies Solis" or "Sunday" for the weekly Christian festival, is in a great measure owing to the union of pagan and Christian sentiment with which the first day of the week was recommended by Constantine to his subjects, pagan and Christian alike, as the "venerable day of the sun". His decree regulating its observance has been justly called a new era in the history of the Lord's Day. It was his mode of harmonizing the discordant religions of the empire under one common institution' (A. P. Stanley, *History of the Eastern Church*, page 184).

History and prophecy are clear on the change of the Bible Sabbath. God did not change the seventh-day Sabbath from Saturday to Sunday. Jesus did not change it, and the first-century disciples would not think of changing the Sabbath. The Sabbath was gradually changed over the centuries as pagan sun worship infiltrated the Church through a union of Church and state in the early centuries.

The Israelites worshipped the Creator on the seventh day of the week, the Bible Sabbath. God's true Church in Revelation 12 keeps all his commandments, including the Sabbath command. The false church revives the Babylonian day of the sun and passes around its cup of false doctrines. Many churches, drinking from that cup, worship on the first day of the week, Sunday.

God has a sign: 'Also I gave them my Sabbaths as a sign between us, so they would know that I the LORD made them holy.' (Ezekiel 20:12.) All through the Old Testament, on into the New Testament, and until the end of time, God's Sabbath is a sign – an everlasting symbol of allegiance to our Creator.

Delusions

The Babylonian teaching of sun worship, that pagan principle passed down from one pagan religion to the next, slipped into the Christian Church, not by a commandment of God, but rather through compromise.

Arthur P. Stanley further states: '[Constantine's] coins bore on the one side the letters of the name of Christ; on the other the figure of the Sun-god . . . as if he could not bear to relinquish the patronage of the bright luminary' (*ibid*). Amazing! On Constantine's coins, Christ's name was written on one side and the sun god was pictured on the other side. A wedding took place between Christianity and paganism, between the Church and the emperor of Rome. Constantine was actually a Christian only in name. As a result, the Christian Church was flooded with many practices that do not find their origins in Scripture. Dr Alexander Hislop says:

'To conciliate the Pagans to nominal Christianity, Rome, pursuing its usual policy, took measures to get the Christian and Pagan festivals amalgamated, and . . . to get Paganism and Christianity – now far sunk in idolatry – in this as in so many other things, *to shake hands*' (*The Two Babylons*, page 105, emphasis supplied).

In other words, Rome was attempting to conciliate, to compromise, to bring the crumbling empire together.

What is the origin of Sunday worship? Where does it come from? How did it enter the Church?

Dr Edward T. Hiscox, author of *The Baptist Manual*, stated in a paper before a Baptist convention of ministers on 13 November 1893: 'There was and is a commandment to keep holy the Sabbath day, but that Sabbath day was not Sunday. . . . It will be said however with some show of triumph, that the Sabbath was transferred from the seventh day to the first day of the week. . . . Where can the record of such a transaction be found? Not in the New Testament –

absolutely not! There is no scriptural evidence of the change of the Sabbath institution from the seventh to the first day of the week. To me [it] seems unaccountable that Jesus, during three years [he spent] with His disciples, often conversing with them on the Sabbath question, never alluded to any transference of the day; also that during forty days of His resurrection life, no such thing was intimated. What a pity that it [Sunday] comes branded with the mark of paganism, and christened with the name of the sun god, then adopted and sanctioned by the papal apostasy, and bequeathed as a sacred legacy to Protestantism!'

The door was opened as Babylonian practices flooded into the Church. A Roman Catholic source says: 'Christendom is indebted to the Catholic Church for the institution of Sunday as the Sabbath day. But there is no precedent in Scripture, nor commandment in Scripture, to observe the Sunday as the Sabbath day' (*Our Sunday Visitor*, 4 January 1931).

In the fourth century, in an attempt to convert the pagans and save the empire, church leaders opened that door. The Roman emperor, Constantine, who had, on the surface become a Christian, walked through that door, and Church and state united. Babylonian sun worship entered the Christian Church as this union between paganism and Christianity took place.

F. G. Lentz says, 'In keeping Sunday, non-Catholics are simply following the practice of the Catholic Church for 1,800 years, a tradition, and not a Bible ordinance' (*The Question Box*, page 99).

After Christ died and the apostles passed off the scene, the Church drifted from its original teachings. Nevertheless, there was a small remnant who remained loyal to God. Down through the ages, God has always had those who have said, 'We will not compromise; we must stand for truth, no matter what the masses are doing. We have submitted our lives to Christ. He has

Delusions

said, "If you love me, you will keep my commandments." (John 14:15, NRSV.) We will take the Word of God as our guide. We will stand loyally for Jesus.'

At times, that remnant was oppressed and persecuted. Still, they would not accept the Babylonian principle of human decrees above the Scriptures. They would not accept the Babylonian principle of an earthly head of the Church rather than Christ. They would not accept the Babylonian principle of images. They worshipped Jesus directly. They would not accept the Babylonian principle that there is an immortal soul which lives on, outside the body. They would not accept the Babylonian principle of sun worship.

It is not hard to identify the woman in scarlet of Revelation 17. Nor is it hard to identify her daughters who have been sipping from her wine cup and accepting her errors. But remember, whatever the denominational label, God offers his salvation to *individuals*. He calls people out of communions in which they are in spiritual danger and leads them to Bible truth.

You may be wondering, 'Can I believe the truth and remain just where I am?' In every world-conforming church, there are members of God's invisible, true Church who, if they would be safe, must come out. God calls you to come out, because Babylon is fallen.

The noted Catholic author, Cardinal Gibbons, wrote: 'Reason and sense demand the acceptance of one or the other of these alternatives: either Protestantism and the keeping holy of Saturday, or Catholicity and the keeping holy of Sunday. *Compromise is impossible*.' (*Catholic Mirror*, 23 December 1893, emphasis supplied.) I agree with Cardinal Gibbons completely on this point. Compromise *is* impossible! These issues are too clear. They demand a choice. This evidence demands a verdict. God is calling men and women to take a stand.

When God said REMEMBER

Listen to the words of Scripture: 'With a mighty voice he shouted: Fallen! Fallen is Babylon the Great!' (Revelation 18:2.) The mother Church is fallen. Her traditions are fallen. All systems that teach error are fallen. They have drifted away from Scripture as the only rule of faith and practice.

'Then I heard another voice from heaven say: Come out of her, my people, so that you will not share in her sins, so that you will not receive any of her plagues' (verse 4). There is no way to stay in Babylon without sharing in her sins. Babylon is fallen! There is no way that you can change her. Your mission, your business, is to come out.

God is calling honest-hearted men and women out of those churches that have drunk the cup of Babylon. Soon time is going to run out. Soon every human being is going to make his or her final choice, fully for Christ or fully for tradition, either on the side of truth or on the side of error, standing with the Scriptures or standing with human beings and human substitutes.

Our only safety is in coming out of every church that is based on tradition, that uses images in its worship, that has sipped the wine cup and is still practising Sunday worship. God's appeal is to come out.

Jesus said, 'My sheep listen to my voice; I know them, and they follow me.' (John 10:27.) He says, 'My child, I am appealing to you. I have my sheep, my followers, in every church. I am appealing to people of all denominations to lay aside their preconceived opinions and follow the Bible. I am speaking to hearts everywhere to come out of those churches based on tradition.'

Oh, I appeal to you, my friends. I appeal to you in Jesus' name to surrender your will to him and to determine to do his will. With your Bible in your hand, tell Jesus, 'I can do no other; I must come out. I hear your call to my heart. I see how paganism and Christianity united in those early centuries. I see the issue very clearly now. I see that for more than eighteen hundred years compromise has taken place. I see that God has been calling his little remnant out, and I have decided to take my stand for you, Lord Jesus. I decide to stand on the Word of God; I decide to stand with Christ. I am willing to come out, even if it means standing alone.'

Oh, friend of mine, will you not settle it in your heart right now? Will you not seal it in your mind? Will you not tell Jesus, 'Lord, I hear your call that Babylon the Great is fallen. I hear you urging, "Come out of her, my people" '?

Tenderly, in tones of love, Jesus, by his Spirit, speaks to your heart. With loving-kindness he says, 'I love you, my child. My child, I am appealing to you right now!' Some of Jesus' people are still in Babylon. Do you hear his call right now? Do you hear him speaking to your heart? I know that, right now, you are willing to say, 'Jesus, I love you and I choose to follow you. Because I love you, I desire to be part of your commandment-keeping people. I hear your voice gently appealing, "If you love me, you will keep my commandments." (John 14:15, NRSV.) Yes, Lord, I will follow.'

---Chapter nine---

Be a trailblazer for God

We thought we'd left 'holy wars' behind in the Middle Ages. They're back with a vengeance.

There are people out there quite willing to bring your world crashing down if they can't have the world their way. They're willing to go up in smoke and to take others with them. And they profess a fierce loyalty to their faith.

How do we know what really expresses allegiance to God? How do we know what issue will divide humanity in the end time?

The Bible gives us clues, and they are clues that cut across the dividing lines of culture and religion.

The third chapter of Daniel presents us with a remarkable scene on the Plain of Dura in ancient Babylon. An enormous gold statue of King Nebuchadnezzar had been set up. Thousands of representatives from his empire had been invited to bow down before it in a splendid ceremony. The king was making a statement. He was saying, 'I will be left standing when other kings and empires have fallen.' Babylon, he was saying, would last forever.

Just as the assembly bowed to the ground towards the image, something interrupted the proceedings. Three young men remained standing. They were three young Jewish princes, Shadrach, Meshach and Abednego. They'd been brought as captives to Babylon and were being trained to help govern its great empire.

Be a trailblazer for God

They stuck out like sore thumbs. Babylonian officials quickly brought Nebuchadnezzar the news. This was treason. The king's herald had made an announcement a few moments before in a loud voice that rang over the plain.

His words are recorded in Daniel: 'Then the herald loudly proclaimed, This is what you are commanded to do. . . . As soon as you hear the sound of the horn, . . . you must fall down and worship the image of gold that King Nebuchadnezzar has set up. Whoever does not fall down and worship will immediately be thrown into a blazing furnace.' (Daniel 3:4-6.)

The king had made this act of worship a test of loyalty. Nebuchadnezzar wanted total allegiance. Well, that put the three Hebrews in a terrible bind. They'd been taught since childhood that there was only one Being worthy of worship. Bowing down to an idol was a betrayal of their faith. And yet, if they didn't bow down, they'd be burned to death!

Tough choice! What would you do in a situation like that? How important are these gestures of allegiance?

Nebuchadnezzar's decree has a striking parallel in the New Testament. Revelation chapter 13 talks about a challenge God's people will face at the end of time. The antichrist sets up an image to his representative, the beast:

'He was given power to give breath to the image of the first beast, so that it could speak and cause all who refused to worship the image to be killed. He also forced everyone, small and great, rich and poor, free and slave, to receive a mark on his right hand or on his forehead, so that no-one could buy or sell unless he had the mark, which is the name of the beast or the number of his name.' (Revelation 13:15-17.)

Notice the parallels between Nebuchadnezzar's decree and the decree in Revelation:

- In both a world leader attempts to compel worship of an image.

- In both there is something that contradicts God's specific commandment to worship him alone.
- In both all who do not submit are condemned to death.

To whom are we going to bow down? That's the ultimate question. At some point, believers are going to be confronted by a great power, a religious and political power that demands our ultimate allegiance. And the issue is worship. There's true worship and false worship.

You know, the theme of worship runs all through the book of Revelation.

The theme comes into sharp focus in the very heart of the book. Revelation 12 and 13 introduce us to symbolic creatures who represent evil forces in the world – the beast, the dragon and the false prophet. They are trying to get everyone to bow down to that image of the beast.

And then, in Revelation 14, we find God's dramatic response to this great challenge, his response to false worship. It is, in fact, the Almighty's final message of warning to the world. It's given by three angels flying in the sky who have an eternal Gospel to proclaim. This is what they say: 'Fear God and give him glory, because the hour of his judgement has come. Worship him who made the heavens, the earth, the sea and the springs of water.' (Revelation 14:7.)

Who is it that we are called to worship? The Creator of Heaven and Earth, the One who breathes life into every creature. Only our Creator has the right to judge us; we are responsible to him and him alone.

True worship focuses on the God who stands above us as Creator and Judge. It's to him that we need to give our allegiance.

The angels of Revelation 14 go on to warn about the terrible fate of those who worship the beast: 'If anyone worships the beast and his image . . . he, too, will drink of the wine of God's fury,' (Revelation 14:9, 10).

Chapter nine
Be a trailblazer for God

Notice that here we see the counterpoint to the first angel's message. We are *not* to worship the beast; we *are* to worship the Creator. These two choices stand in opposition. The one calls us into a false allegiance to something man-made. The other calls us to give God glory, to worship him as Creator.

Worshipping the beast is deadly. So how do we stand against it when pressured to conform? How do we keep from worshipping its image? By fixing an unconditional faith on our Creator. His authority must supersede all others.

God has given us a way to express our unconditional allegiance to the Creator regularly, every week. It is evidence of our commitment to him as our Creator and Lord. It's found in the fourth commandment. This is something many Christians have overlooked: 'Remember the Sabbath day, to keep it holy. Six days you shall labour and do all your work, but the seventh day is the Sabbath of the LORD your God. In it you shall do no work: you, nor your son, nor your daughter, nor your male servant, nor your female servant, nor your cattle, nor your stranger who is within your gates. For in six days the LORD made the heavens and the earth, the sea, and all that is in them, and rested the seventh day. Therefore the LORD blessed the Sabbath day and hallowed it.' (Exodus 20:8-11, NKJV.)

Why are we urged to observe the seventh day, Saturday? Because it's a memorial of Creation. It ties us to our Creator. It's a rest in God's finished work. The fourth commandment asks us to remember the One who made the heavens and the earth.

The Sabbath, then, is a symbol of our love and loyalty to our Creator. Think again of that decree of the antichrist in Revelation, the decree that demands that everyone bow down to the image of the beast – on pain of death.

The Bible's last book, Revelation, outlines a time of

end-time crisis. God's followers will be confronted with a choice between the commandments of God and the tyranny of enforced worship.

So we need to make sure we're worshipping the right God in the right way. That's the issue. Those three young Hebrews standing on the Plain of Dura understood that well. Let's return to their story.

King Nebuchadnezzar was outraged, of course, that anyone would interrupt his moment of glory. He had the three brought before him. He pointed to the blazing furnace. He asked, very pointedly, 'What god will be able to rescue you from my hand?' (Daniel 3:15.)

The answer these Hebrew youths gave is justly famous. Fearlessly they replied to the king, 'O Nebuchadnezzar, . . . If we are thrown into the blazing furnace, the God we serve is able to save us from it, . . . But even if he does not, we want you to know, O king, that we will not serve your gods or worship the image of gold you have set up.' (Daniel 3:16-18.)

These men answered the proud king's challenge without hesitation. They did so by testifying of their faith in the God of Heaven and Earth. They were committed to worshipping him alone, even if he did not deliver them from death.

And what was the result? An enraged Nebuchadnezzar had his furnace fired up to the maximum. Then he had the Hebrews thrown into the flames. Apparently their God was not going to save them.

But he did. In fact, he made a wonderful appearance, right in the midst of that fiery furnace. Nebuchadnezzar was astonished to observe a fourth figure in the furnace. He cried out, 'I see four men loose, walking in the midst of the fire; and they are not hurt, and the form of the fourth is like the Son of God.' (Daniel 3:25, NKJV.)

Three men had been thrown in. But four were alive and well in that furnace! Shadrach, Meshach and

Be a trailblazer for God

Abednego were walking in the flames in company with the Son of God.

You know, the book of Daniel teaches us something important – the final crisis outlined in the book of Revelation need not terrify us. It can be an opportunity for us to see our Lord, very close and very powerful. These young Hebrews had their eyes fixed on a great God. And in their hour of trial, they found that a great God had come to be with them. That's what an unconditional faith, a committed faith, can do for us. It will bring God close in the worst of times.

Those three Hebrews in the fiery furnace made quite an impression, too. King Nebuchadnezzar called to them to come out. As they emerged, a large crowd gathered. They noticed that their hair wasn't even singed. Their clothes didn't even smell of smoke.

Ultimately, that fiery trial the Hebrews went through burned only one thing – the ropes that bound them. Shadrach, Meshach and Abednego came out of the furnace conquerors.

For the first time, King Nebuchadnezzar knew that there was a God in Heaven far bigger than he could ever be. He acknowledged that these three Hebrews were 'servants of the Most High God'. Up to this point, the king had tried to be the most high himself, with his massive golden statue.

But now, he made a remarkable confession. We find it in Daniel chapter 3: 'Praise be to the God of Shadrach, Meshach and Abednego, who has sent his angel and rescued his servants! They trusted in him and defied the king's command and were willing to give up their lives rather than serve or worship any god except their own God.' (Daniel 3:28.)

Nebuchadnezzar's rage had turned to reverence. He realised that another kind of allegiance was important. He realised that he needed to worship the right God in the right way. He needed to bow before the God who comes close in times of trouble.

That's the God who deserves our allegiance today.

History is headed towards a climax. There will be a choice of allegiance. We shall either worship the Creator or we shall worship something man-made. We shall either worship the Lord of Heaven and Earth or we shall worship someone who promises us Heaven on Earth. We shall either place our faith in the invisible, holy God or we shall be captured by the dazzle of an image. We'll either stand for his truth or we shall be swept up by the crowd.

'Blessed are those who do his commandments, that they may have the right to the tree of life, and may enter through the gates into the city.' (Revelation 22:14, NKJV.)

In small ways and in big ways, the battle lines are being drawn. Hate is disguised as religious fervour. 'My side', 'my tradition' replaces the law of God. Battle lines are being drawn right now between the empire of Satan and the empire of Christ.

Where's our allegiance? Do we bow before Someone greater and grander than us? Or do we bow before an image we make – an image that suits our prejudice, our tradition, our private truth?

I want to stand with the three brave Hebrews. I want to stand with them in the time of the end. And I believe their kind of faith is available to each and every one of us, a faith that will stand tall when times get rough. It's really a matter of perspective. What do we choose to place at the centre of our lives? Who gets first place? Whose truth gets top priority?

Please make sure you remember the Creator each Sabbath. Take time now before the clash of allegiances makes it too late. Sabbath worship will transform your life. It will build up your faith before the crisis breaks.

The Creator, the Lord, the Judge, the Lawgiver, the Redeemer, the One who loves us to the uttermost – he alone deserves our worship. The Sabbath stands as a great symbol of our commitment to our Creator. There

Be a trailblazer for God

are many counterfeits but only one Creator God, and the Sabbath calls all humanity back to him.

As you read these pages have you sensed God leading you to a deeper, fuller experience with him? Has the Holy Spirit convicted you of the truth of the Bible Sabbath? If you are convinced of what God wants you to do, now is the time to act.

Happiness comes from knowing and doing the will of God. As you put the Sabbath into practice in your own life and worship each week with God's people, you will be immeasurably blessed. You will draw nearer to Jesus than you ever imagined possible.

I realise that change always brings a measure of difficulty. Long cherished ideas and worship patterns are difficult to change. Simply because we have believed something to be true and practised it for years does not make it true. Throughout the history of Christianity God has challenged his people to follow truth, even if it be contrary to the prevailing culture. The majority is not always right. God values truth more than majority opinion. His commandments are the basis of morality and the foundation of his throne.

I urge you to consider the truth of the Bible Sabbath seriously. If God is calling you to make a change in your life, have the courage to do it. Be a trailblazer for God. Set the pace for others to follow. God will bless your family and friends through you as you step out to follow him. You will have a deep inner satisfaction in doing what is right because it is right. You will join millions of others in keeping God's special day as you heed the Master's call to 'Remember the Sabbath day', and for you the Sabbath will no longer be the Almost Forgotten Commandment.

When **God** said
REMEMBER

Father, we acknowledge you as our Creator and as our Redeemer. Thank you that, no matter how overwhelming the conflict might seem, you are able to deliver. We know that times are coming when our allegiance will be tested. But we know that you can make us loyal and courageous and true. We place our trust in you as that kind of God. In Jesus' name, Amen.